Fuzzy Mitten's
Fuzzy Knits

by Barbara Prime

Table of Contents

3	Polar Bear
5	Pupster
9	Silly Duck
13	Fuzzy Lamb
18	Mister Bunny
21	Chipmunk
25	Siamese Kitty
30	Tiger
33	Mouse
37	Panda
40	Monkey
44	Pug
48	Abbreviations

Polar Bear
with a Cardigan

BEAR

Materials
50 g of cream worsted weight yarn, black yarn for embroidering face, two 8-10 mm black buttons or safety eyes, stuffing, pair of 4 mm (US size 6) knitting needles, tapestry needle

Measurements
Approx. 20 cm (8") tall

Gauge/Tension
22 sts and 32 rows per 10 cm (4")

Legs (make 2)
Begin at sole. CO 10 sts.

Row 1: P 1 row.
Row 2: k1, [m1, k1] to end. (19 sts)
Row 3: P 1 row.
Row 4: k4, [m1, k3] x 5. (24 sts)
Row 5-7: work 3 rows in st st.
Row 8: k8, [skpo] x 2, [k2tog] x 2, k8. (20 sts)
Row 9: p6, [p2tog] x 2, [p2tog tbl] x 2, p6. (16 sts)
Row 10: k7, k2tog, k7. (15 sts)
Row 11-13: work 3 rows in st st.
Row 14: k2, m1, k11, m1, k2. (17 sts)
Row 15-25: work 11 rows in st st.
Row 26: k1, [k2tog] x 8. (9 sts)

Cut yarn, thread end through remaining sts, pull tight to gather. Sew up sole and back leg seam, leaving an opening. Stuff and sew closed.

Body
Begin at neck. CO 16 sts.

Row 1: P 1 row.
Row 2: k1, [m1, k1] to end. (31 sts)
Row 3-5: work 3 rows in st st.
Row 6: k8, m1, k15, m1, k8. (33 sts)
Row 7-13: work 7 rows in st st.
Row 14: k15, m1, k3, m1, k15. (35 sts)
Row 15-17: work 3 rows in st st.
Row 18: k3, m1, k1, m1, k27, m1, k1, m1, k3. (39 sts)
Row 19: P 1 row.
Row 20: k16, skpo, k3, k2tog, k16. (37 sts)
Row 21-23: work 3 rows in st st.
Row 24: k15, skpo, k3, k2tog, k15. (35 sts)
Row 25-27: work 3 rows in st st.
Row 28: k1, [k2tog] to end. (18 sts)
Row 29: P 1 row.
Row 30: [k2tog] x 9. (9 sts)

Cut yarn, thread end through remaining sts, pull tight to gather. Sew up back seam to neck edge (leaving cast-on edge open). Stuff body.

Right arm
Begin at paw. CO 6 sts.

Row 1: P 1 row.
Row 2: k1, [m1, k1] to end. (11 sts)
Row 3: P 1 row.
Row 4: [k2, m1] x 2, k3, [m1, k2] x 2. (15 sts)
Row 5-7: work 3 rows in st st.
Row 8: k1, [skpo] x 2, [k2tog] x 2, k6. (11 sts)
Row 9-13: work 5 rows in st st.
Row 14: k5, [m1, k3] x 2. (13 sts)
Row 15-23: work 9 rows in st st.
Row 24: k1, [k2tog] x 6. (7 sts)

Cut yarn, thread end through remaining sts, pull tight to gather. Sew up seam, leaving an opening. Stuff and sew closed.

Left arm
Begin at paw. CO 6 sts.

Row 1: P 1 row.
Row 2: k1, [m1, k1] to end. (11 sts)
Row 3: P 1 row.
Row 4: [k2, m1] x 2, k3, [m1, k2] x 2. (15 sts)
Row 5-7: work 3 rows in st st.
Row 8: k6, [skpo] x 2, [k2tog] x 2, k1. (11 sts)
Row 9-13: work 5 rows in st st.
Row 14: [k3, m1] x 2, k5. (13 sts)
Row 15-23: work 9 rows in st st.
Row 24: k1, [k2tog] x 6. (7 sts)

Finish same as right arm.

Head

Begin at back. CO 7 sts.

Row 1: P 1 row.
Row 2: k1, [m1, k1] to end. (13 sts)
Row 3: P 1 row.
Row 4: k1, [m1, k1] to end. (25 sts)
Row 5-7: work 3 rows in st st.
Row 8: [k2, m1] x 4, k9, [m1, k2] x 4. (33 sts)
Row 9-19: work 11 rows in st st.
Row 20: k8, [skpo] x 2, k9, [k2tog] x 2, k8. (29 sts)
Row 21: P 1 row.
Row 22: k1, [skpo] x 6, k3, [k2tog] x 6, k1. (17 sts)
Row 23-29: work 7 rows in st st.
Row 30: k1, [k2tog] x 8. (9 sts)

Cut yarn, thread end through remaining sts, pull tight to gather. Attach safety eyes. Sew up seam, leaving an opening. Stuff and sew closed. Make sure to put extra stuffing in the nose and cheeks.

Ears (make 2)

CO 3 sts.

Row 1: P 1 row.
Row 2: k1, [m1, k1] x 2. (5 sts)
Row 3: P 1 row.
Row 4: k1, [m1, k1] x 4. (9 sts)
Row 5: P 1 row.
Row 6: k4, m1, k1, m1, k4. (11 sts)
Row 7-9: P 3 rows.
Row 10: k3, skpo, k1, k2tog, k3. (9 sts)
Row 11: P 1 row.
Row 12: [skpo] x 2, k1, [k2tog] x 2. (5 sts)
Row 13: P 1 row.
Row 14: skpo, k1, k2tog. (3 sts)

Cut yarn, thread end through remaining sts, pull tight to gather. Fold ear in half, with decreases to front and increases to back.

Finishing

If not using safety eyes, sew on button eyes or embroider eyes with black yarn. With length of black yarn, embroider nose and mouth. Sew ears onto head (purl ridge is upper ear edge). Sew head securely to cast-on edge of body. Thread a length of yarn through left arm about 1 cm (¼") from top, thread yarn through body at shoulder position, then thread yarn through right arm. Thread yarn through body again, and then the left arm and pull tight. Repeat so yarn passes through each arm 3-4 times. Pull yarn tight so arms are secure, then fasten off yarn. Attach legs at lower edge of body in the same way as the arms.

MOSS-STITCH CARDIGAN

Materials

25 g of worsted/aran weight yarn, pair of 4.5 mm (US size 7) knitting needles, 4 small buttons, tapestry needle, scrap yarn

Measurements

22 cm (8½") around, 10 cm (4") long

Gauge/Tension

20 sts and 28 rows per 10 cm (4") in moss st

Moss stitch pattern

Rows 1 & 2: [k1, p1] to end.
Rows 3 & 4: [p1, k1] to end.

Back

CO 22 sts.

Row 1-13: work 13 rows in moss st
Row 14: k1, p3tog, [k1, p1] x 7, k3tog, p1. (18 sts)

Mark each end of row 14.

Row 15-25: work 11 rows in moss st.
Row 26: bind off 4 sts, work 10 sts in moss st, bind off 4 sts.

Cut yarn. Place the 10 sts on scrap yarn.

Left Front

CO 12 sts.

Row 1-13: work 13 rows in moss st

Row 14: k1, p3tog, [k1, p1] x 4. (10 sts)

Mark beginning of row 14.

Row 15-25: work 11 rows in moss st.
Row 26: bind off 4 sts, work 6 sts in moss st.

Cut yarn. Place 6 sts on scrap yarn

Right Front

CO 12 sts.

Row 1: work row 1 of moss st.
Row 2: k2tog, yo, [k1, p1] x 5.
Row 3-8: work 6 rows in moss st.
Row 9: [k1, p1] x 5, yo, p2tog.
Row 10-13: work 3 rows in moss st.
Row 14: [k1, p1] x 4, k3tog, k1. (10 sts)

Mark end of row 14.

Row 15: [p1, k1] x 5.
Row 16: p2tog, yo, [p1, k1] x 4.
Row 17-22: work these 6 rows in moss st.
Row 23: [p1, k1] x 4, yo, k2tog.
Row 24-25: work these 2 rows in moss st.

Row 26: [k1, p1] x3, bind off 4 sts.

Cut yarn. Place 6 sts on scrap yarn. Sew fronts to back along shoulder seams.

Collar

Place 22 sts for collar onto needle, so RS is ready to knit.

Row 1: skpo, [p1, k1] x 9, k2tog. (20 sts)
Row 2: p2tog, [k1, p1] x 8, p2tog tbl. (18 sts)
Row 3: bind off loosely in pattern.

Cut yarn, secure yarn ends.

Sleeves

With RS of garment facing you, pick up 16 sts between markers on front and back.

Row 1-9: work 9 rows in moss st.
Row 10: bind off in pattern.

Sew together sleeve and side seams. Sew buttons onto left front, using button-holes on right front as a guide for placement.

• •

PUPSTER

Materials

40 g of brown (MC) worsted weight yarn, 15 g of cream (CC) worsted weight yarn, black yarn for embroidery, two 8-10 mm buttons or safety eyes, stuffing, pair of 4 mm (US size 6) knitting needles, tapestry needle

Measurements

Approx. 20 cm (8") tall

Gauge/Tension

22 sts and 32 rows per 10 cm (4")

Legs (make 2)

Begin at sole. CO 10 sts with CC.

Row 1: P 1 row.
Row 2: k1, [m1, k1] to end. (19 sts)
Row 3: P 1 row.

Row 4: k4, [m1, k3] x 5. (24 sts)
Row 5-7: work 3 rows in st st.
Row 8: k8, [skpo] x 2, [k2tog] x 2, k8. (20 sts)
Row 9: p6, [p2tog] x 2, [p2tog tbl] x 2, p6. (16 sts)
Row 10: k7, k2tog, k7. (15 sts)
Row 11-13: work 3 rows in st st.
Row 14: k2, m1, k11, m1, k2. (17 sts)

Break off CC and start next row with MC.

Row 15-25: work 11 rows in st st.
Row 26: k1, [k2tog] 8 times. (9 sts)

Cut yarn, thread end through remaining sts, pull tight to gather. Sew up sole and back leg seam, leaving an opening. Stuff and sew closed.

Body

Begin at neck. CO 16 sts with MC.

Row 1: P 1 row.
Row 2: k1, [m1, k1] to end. (31 sts)

PUPSTER
WITH A HEART PULLOVER

Row 3-5: work 3 rows in st st.
Row 6: k8, m1, k15, m1, k8. (33 sts)
Row 7-13: work 7 rows in st st.
Row 14: k15, m1, k3, m1, k15. (35 sts)
Row 15-17: work 3 rows in st st.
Row 18: k3, m1, k1, m1, k27, m1, k1, m1, k3. (39 sts)
Row 19: P 1 row.
Row 20: k16, skpo, k3, k2tog, k16. (37 sts)
Row 21-23: work 3 rows in st st.
Row 24: k15, skpo, k3, k2tog, k15. (35 sts)
Row 25-27: work 3 rows in st st.
Row 28: k1, [k2tog] to end. (18 sts)
Row 29: P 1 row.
Row 30: [k2tog] x 9. (9 sts)

Cut yarn, thread end through remaining sts, pull tight to gather. Sew up back seam to neck edge (leaving cast-on edge open). Stuff body.

Right arm

Begin at paw. CO 6 sts with CC.

Row 1: P 1 row.
Row 2: k1, [m1, k1] to end. (11 sts)
Row 3: P 1 row.
Row 4: [k2, m1] x 2, k3, [m1, k2] x 2. (15 sts)
Row 5-7: work 3 rows in st st.
Row 8: k1, [skpo] x 2, [k2tog] x 2, k6. (11 sts)
Row 9-11: work 3 rows in st st.

Break off CC and start next row with MC.

Row 12-13: work 2 rows in st st.
Row 14: k5, [m1, k3] x 2. (13 sts)
Row 15-23: work 8 rows in st st.
Row 24: k1, [k2tog] x 6. (7 sts)

Cut yarn, thread end through remaining sts, pull tight to gather. Sew up seam, leaving an opening. Stuff and sew closed.

Left Arm

Begin at paw. CO 6 sts with CC.

Row 1: P 1 row.
Row 2: k1, [m1, k1] to end. (11 sts)
Row 3: P 1 row.
Row 4: [k2, m1] x 2, k3, [m1, k2] x 2. (15 sts)
Row 5-7: work 3 rows in st st.
Row 8: k6, [skpo] x 2, [k2tog] x 2, k1. (11 sts)
Row 9-11: work 3 rows in st st.

Break off CC and start next row with MC.

Row 12-13: work 2 rows in st st.
Row 14: [k3, m1] x 2, k5. (13 sts)
Row 15-23: work 8 rows in st st.
Row 24: k1, [k2tog] x 6. (7 sts)

Finish same as right arm.

Head

The intarsia section is marked with the yarn colour for each set of sts.

Begin at back. CO 7 sts with MC.

Row 1: P 1 row.
Row 2: k1, [m1, k1] to end. (13 sts)
Row 3: P 1 row.
Row 4: k1, [m1, k1] to end. (25 sts)
Row 5-7: work 3 rows in st st.
Row 8: [k2, m1] x 4, k9, [m1, k2] x 4. (33 sts)
Row 9-16: work 8 rows in st st.
Row 17: MC p16, CC p1, MC p16.
Row 18: MC k15, CC k3, MC k15.
Row 19: MC p14, CC p5, MC p14.
Row 20: MC k13, CC k7, MC k13.

Work rest of nose in CC.

Row 21: P 1 row.
Row 22: [skpo] x 8, k3, [k2tog] x 8. (17 sts)
Row 23-27: work 5 rows in st st.
Row 28: k1, [k2tog] x 8. (9 sts)

Cut yarn, thread end through remaining sts, pull tight to gather. Secure yarn ends from colour changes. Attach safety eyes. Sew up seam, leaving an opening. Stuff and sew closed. Make sure to put extra stuffing in the nose and cheeks.

Ears (make 2)

CO 3 sts with MC.

Row 1: K 1 row.
Row 2: k1, [m1, k1] x 2. (5 sts).
Row 3: K 1 row.
Row 4: k1, m1, k to end. (6 sts)
Row 5: K 1 row.
Row 6-11: repeat rows 4-5 x 3. (9 sts)
Row 12-25: knit 14 rows in garter st.
Row 26: k1, skpo, k to last 3 sts, k2tog, k1. (7 sts)
Row 27: K 1 row.
Row 28-29: repeat rows 26-27. (5 sts)
Row 30: k1, sl, k2tog, psso, k1. (3 sts)
Row 31: K 1 row.

Cut yarn, thread end through remaining sts, pull tight to gather. Secure yarn end.

Tail

CO 10 sts with MC.

Work in st st for 5 cm (2") ending in RS row. Switch to CC, P 1 row.

Next: [k1, k2tog] x 3, k1. (7 sts) P 1 row.
Next: [k2tog] x 3, k1. (4 sts)

Cut yarn, thread end through remaining sts, pull tight to gather. Sew seam, stuffing lightly as you sew.

Finishing

If not using safety eyes, sew on button eyes or embroider eyes with black yarn. With length of yarn, embroider nose and mouth. Sew ears onto head (edge with increases is sewn to head). Sew head securely to cast-on edge of body. Thread a length of yarn through left arm about 1 cm (¼") from top, thread yarn through body at shoulder position, then thread yarn through right arm. Thread yarn through body again, and then the left arm and pull tight. Repeat so yarn passes through each arm 3-4 times. Pull yarn tight so arms are secure, then fasten off yarn. Attach legs at lower edge of body in the same way as the arms. Sew tail to puppy's bum.

HEART PULLOVER

Materials

25 g of DK weight yarn, pair of 3.75 mm (US size 5) knitting needles, scrap yarn, tapestry needle

Size

19 cm (7½") around, 6 cm (2½") long

Gauge/Tension

22 sts and 32 rows per 10 cm (4")

Back

CO 27 sts.

Row 1-3: k1, [p1, k1] to end.
Row 4-13: beginning with K row, work 10 rows in st st.
Row 14: k1, k3tog tbl, k19, k3tog, k1. (23 sts)

Mark each end of row 14.

Row 15-25: work 11 rows in st st.
Row 26: k6, [p1, k1] x 6, k5.
Row 27: p5, bind off 13 sts, p5. Or, bind off all sts.

Cut yarn. Place remaining 13 sts on scrap yarn.

Front

CO 27 sts.

Row 1-3: k1, [p1, k1] to end.
Row 4-9: beginning with K row, work 6 rows in st st.
Row 10: k12, k2tog, yo, k13.
Row 11: P 1 row.
Row 12: k11, k2tog, yo, k1, yo, ssk, k11.
Row 13: P 1 row.
Row 14: k1, k3tog tbl, k6, k2tog, yo, k3, yo, ssk, k6, k3tog, k1. (23 sts)

Mark each end of row 14.

Row 15: P 1 row.
Row 16: k7, k2tog, yo, k5, yo, ssk, k7.
Row 17: P 1 row.

Row 18: k6, k2tog, yo, k2, k2tog, yo, k3, yo, ssk, k6.
Row 19: P 1 row.
Row 20: k8, [yo, s1, k2tog, psso, yo, k1] x 2, k7.
Row 21-25: work 5 rows in st st.
Row 26: k6, [p1, k1] x 6, k5.
Row 27: p5, bind off 13 sts, p5. Or, bind off all sts.

Place remaining 13 sts on scrap yarn. Graft or sew together shoulder seams and secure yarn ends.

Sleeves

With RS facing you, pick up 21 sts between markers on front and back.

Row 1-10: work 10 rows in st st.
Row 11-12: k1, [p1, k1] to end.
Row 13: bind off in pattern.

Sew together underarm and side seams. Secure all yarn ends.

Pupster is wearing scarf from Silly Duck pattern, knit in mohair yarn.

• •

DUCK

Materials

40 g of worsted weight yarn in main colour (MC), 15 g of worsted weight yarn in contrasting colour (CC), two 8-10 mm black buttons or safety eyes, stuffing, pair of 4 mm knitting needles (US size 6), tapestry needle

Measurements

Approx. 18 cm (7") tall

Gauge/Tension

22 sts and 28 rows to 10 cm (4")

Legs (make 2)

CO 11 sts with CC.

Row 1: P 1 row.
Row 2: k1, [m1, k1] to end. (21 sts)
Row 3: P 1 row.
Row 4: k6, [m1, k2] x 6, k3. (27 sts)
Row 5-9: work 5 rows in st st.
Row 10: k4, [skpo, k1] x 3, k1, [k1, k2tog] x 3, k4. (21 sts)
Row 11: p4, [p2tog] x 3, p1, [p2tog tbl] x 3, p4. (15 sts)
Row 12: k6, k3tog, k6. (13 sts)
Row 13-15: work 3 rows in st st.
Row 16: [k1, skpo] x 2, k1, [k2tog, k1] x 2. (9 sts)

Bind off. Sew sole and back leg seam, leaving bound-off edge open. Stuff leg, but not foot. Flatten foot and stitch top of foot to bottom with 2 lines of running stitch, starting from ankle and ending at toe edge (making a V with point at ankle).

Body

Begin at neck. CO 16 sts with MC.

Row 1: P 1 row.
Row 2: [k2, m1, k2] x 4. (20 sts)
Row 3-7: work 5 rows in st st.
Row 8: [k1, m1, k1] x 10. (30 sts)
Row 9-11: work 3 rows in st st.
Row 12: k8, m1, k7, m1, k7, m1, k8. (33 sts)
Row 13-15: work 3 rows in st st.
Row 16: k15, m1, k3, m1, k15. (35 sts)
Row 17: P 1 row.
Row 18: k3, m1, k1, m1, k27, m1, k1, m1, k3. (39 sts)
Row 19-21: work 3 rows in st st.
Row 22: [k3, m1] x 2, k27, [m1, k3] x 2. (43 sts)
Row 23: P 1 row.
Row 24: k16, skpo, k7, k2tog, k16. (41 sts)
Row 25: P 1 row.
Row 26: k16, skpo, k5, k2tog, k16. (39 sts)
Row 27: P 1 row.
Row 28: k16, skpo, k3, k2tog, k16.

SILLY DUCK
WITH A HAT AND A SCARF

(37 sts)
Row 29: P 1 row.
Row 30: k16, skpo, k1, k2tog, k16. (35 sts)
Row 31: P 1 row.
Row 32: K1, [k2tog] to end. (18 sts)
Row 33: P 1 row.
Row 34: [k2tog] x 9. (9 sts)

Cut yarn, thread end through remaining sts, pull tight to gather. Sew up back seam to neck edge (leaving cast-on edge open). Stuff body.

Right wing

CO 7 sts with MC.

Row 1: P 1 row.
Row 2: k1 [m1, k1] to end. (13 sts)
Row 3: P 1 row.
Row 4: k1, [p1, k1] to end.
Row 5: P 1 row.
Row 6: skpo, k1, [p1, k1] to end. (12 sts)
Row 7: P 1 row.
Row 8: skpo, [p1, k1] to end. (11 sts)
Row 9: P 1 row.
Row 10-25: repeat rows 6-9 x 4. (3 sts)

Cut yarn, thread end through remaining sts, pull tight to gather. Secure yarn end.

Left wing

CO 7 sts with MC.

Row 1: P 1 row.
Row 2: k1 [m1, k1] to end. (13 sts)
Row 3: P 1 row.
Row 4: k1, [p1, k1] across.
Row 5: P 1 row.
Row 6: k1, [p1, k1] to last 2 sts, k2tog. (12 sts)
Row 7: P 1 row.
Row 8: [k1, p1] to last 2 sts, k2tog. (11 sts)
Row 9: P 1 row.
Row 10-25: repeat rows 6-9 x 4. (3 sts)

Finish same as right wing.

Head

Begin at back. CO 7 sts with MC.

Row 1: P 1 row.
Row 2: k1, [m1, k1] to end. (13 sts)
Row 3: P 1 row.
Row 4: k1, [m1, k1] to end. (25 sts)
Row 5-9: work 5 rows in st st.
Row 10: k3, [k1, m1] x 4, k11, [m1, k1] x 4, k3. (33 sts)
Row 11-19: work 9 rows in st st.
Row 20: k3, [skpo, k1] x 3, k9, [k1, k2tog] x 3, k3. (27 sts)
Row 21-23: work 3 rows in st st.
Row 24: k1, [k2tog] to end. (14 sts)
Row 25: P 1 row.
Row 26: [k2tog] x 7. (7 sts)

Cut yarn, thread end through remaining sts, pull tight to gather. Attach safety eyes. Sew up seam, leaving an opening. Stuff and sew closed. Make sure to put extra stuffing in the cheeks.

Beak

CO 25 sts with CC.

Row 1: P 1 row.
Row 2: k5, k2tog, k4, s2 as if to k2tog, k1, psso, k4, skpo, k5. (21 sts)
Row 3: P 1 row.
Row 4: k4, k2tog, k9, skpo, k4. (19 sts)
Row 5: p3, p2tog tbl, p9, p2tog, p3. (17 sts)
Row 6: k2, k2tog, k9, skpo, k2. (15 sts)
Row 7: P 1 row.
Row 8: k1, [k2tog] x 3, k1, [skpo] x 3, k1. (9 sts)

Cut yarn, thread end through remaining sts, pull tight to gather. Sew seam along underside of beak. Stuff lightly.

Tail

CO 11 sts with MC.

Row 1: P 1 row.
Row 2: k1, [p1, k1] to end.
Row 3: P 1 row.
Row 4: skpo, k1, [p1, k1] x 3, k2tog. (9 sts)
Row 5: P 1 row.
Row 6: skpo, [p1, k1] x 2, p1, k2tog. (7 sts)

Row 7: P 1 row.
Row 8: skpo, k1, p1, k1, k2tog. (5 sts)
Bind off.

Finishing

If not using safety eyes, sew on button eyes or embroider eyes with black yarn. Sew beak to head, with beak centered where you gathered sts when finishing head. Sew head securely to cast-on edge of body. Sew cast-on edge of wings at shoulder position on the body. Sew top edge of legs to underside of body. Sew cast-on edge of tail to duck's bum.

HAT & SCARF

Materials

Hat: 5-10 g of worsted weight yarn, set of 4.5 mm dpns (US size 7), button or pom-pom
Scarf: 5-10 g of worsted weight yarn, pair of 4.5 mm needles (US size 7)

Measurements

Hat: 16 cm (6½") around, 5.5 cm (2") deep
Scarf: 30 cm (12") long

Gauge/Tension

16 sts and 26 rows per 10 cm (4")

Hat

CO 32 sts. Place 10 sts on each of first 2 needles, and 12 sts on third needle. Join in the round.

Row 1-3: [k1, p1] to end.
Row 4-13: work 10 rows in st st.

You can add stripes in this section if you like.

Row 14: [k2, k2tog] x 8. (24 sts)
Row 15: K 1 row.
Row 16: [k1, k2tog] x 8. (16 sts)
Row 17: K 1 row.
Row 18: [k2tog] x 8. (8 sts)

Cut yarn, thread end through remaining sts, pull tight to gather. Secure yarn end. Add button or pom-pom to hat top.

Scarf

CO 63 sts.

Row 1: p3, [k3, p3] to end.
Row 2: k3, [p3, k3] to end.
Row 3-4: repeat rows 1-2.
Row 5: Bind off in pattern.

Secure yarn ends. Add fringe to scarf ends if you like (see Pupster photo).

Tip time!

A diagram for how to attach the arms and legs. Follow the directions of the arrows, making the stitch across the top of the arm or leg horizontal, rather than vertical as it seems in the diagram. Do this 3-4 times, snugging up the yarn with each pass through the body so the pieces are firmly attached. Then secure the yarn ends.

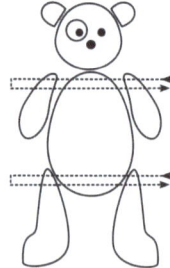

FUZZY LAMB

Materials
40 g of fuzzy worsted weight yarn (MC), 15 g of contrasting worsted weight yarn (CC), yarn for embroidering face, two 8-10 mm black buttons or safety eyes, stuffing, pair of 4 mm (US size 6) knitting needles, tapestry needle

Measurements
Approx. 20 cm (8") tall

Gauge/Tension
22 sts and 32 rows per 10 cm (4")

Legs (make 2)
Begin at sole. CO 10 sts with CC.

Row 1: P 1 row.
Row 2: k1, [m1, k1] to end. (19 sts)
Row 3: P 1 row.
Row 4: k4, [m1, k3] x 5. (24 sts)
Row 5: P 1 row.

Break off CC, start next row with MC.

Row 6-7: work 2 rows in st st.
Row 8: k8, [skpo] x 2, [k2tog] x 2, k8. (20 sts)
Row 9: p6, [p2tog] x 2, [p2tog tbl] x 2, p6. (16 sts)
Row 10: k7, k2tog, k7. (15 sts)
Row 11-13: work 3 rows in st st.
Row 14: k2, m1, k11, m1, k2. (17 sts)
Row 15-25: work 11 rows in st st.
Row 26: k1, [k2tog] x 8. (9 sts)

Cut yarn, thread end through remaining sts, pull tight to gather. Sew sole and back leg seam, leaving an opening. Stuff and sew closed.

Body
Begin at neck. CO 16 sts with MC.

Row 1: P 1 row.
Row 2: k1, [m1, k1] to end. (31 sts)
Row 3-5: work 3 rows in st st.
Row 6: k8, m1, k15, m1, k8. (33 sts)
Row 7-13: work 7 rows in st st.
Row 14: k15, m1, k3, m1, k15. (35 sts)
Row 15-17: work 3 rows in st st.
Row 18: k3, m1, k1, m1, k27, m1, k1, m1, k3. (39 sts)
Row 19: P 1 row.
Row 20: k16, skpo, k3, k2tog, k16. (37 sts)
Row 21-23: work 3 rows in st st.
Row 24: k15, skpo, k3, k2tog, k15. (35 sts)
Row 25-27: work 3 rows in st st.
Row 28: k1, [k2tog] to end. (18 sts)
Row 29: P 1 row.
Row 30: [k2tog] x 9. (9 sts)

Cut yarn, thread end through remaining sts, pull tight to gather. Sew up back seam to neck edge (leaving cast-on edge open). Stuff body.

Right arm
Begin at paw. CO 6 sts with CC.

Row 1: P 1 row.
Row 2: k1, [m1, k1] to end. (11 sts)
Row 3: P 1 row.
Row 4: [k2, m1] x 2, k3, [m1, k2] x 2. (15 sts)
Row 5: P 1 row.

Break off CC, start next row with MC.

Row 6-7: work 2 rows in st st.
Row 8: k1, [skpo] x 2, [k2tog] x 2, k6. (11 sts)
Row 9-13: work 5 rows in st st.
Row 14: k5, [m1, k3] x 2. (13 sts)
Row 15-23: work 9 rows in st st.
Row 24: k1, [k2tog] x 6. (7 sts)

Cut yarn, thread end through remaining sts, pull tight to gather. Sew up seam, leaving an opening. Stuff and sew closed.

Left arm
Begin at paw. CO 6 sts with CC.

Row 1: P 1 row.
Row 2: k1, [m1, k1] to end. (11 sts)
Row 3: P 1 row.
Row 4: [k2, m1] x 2, k3, [m1, k2] x 2. (15 sts)

Fuzzy Lamb
with a Hooded Cardigan

Row 5: P 1 row.

Break off CC, start next row with MC.

Row 6-7: work 2 rows in st st.

Row 8: k6, [skpo] x 2, [k2tog] x 2, k1. (11 sts)

Row 9-13: work 5 rows in st st.

Row 14: [k3, m1] x 2, k5. (13 sts)

Row 15-23: work 9 rows in st st.

Row 24: k1, [k2tog] x 6. (7 sts)

Finish same as right arm.

Head

Begin at back. CO 7 sts with MC.

Row 1: P 1 row.

Row 2: k1, [m1, k1] to end. (13 sts)

Row 3: P 1 row.

Row 4: k1, [m1, k1] to end. (25 sts)

Row 5-7: work 3 rows in st st.

Row 8: [k2, m1] x 4, k9, [m1, k2] x 4. (33 sts)

Row 9-17: work 9 rows in st st.

Break off MC, start next row with CC.

Row 18-19: work 2 rows in st st.

Row 20: k8, [skpo] x 2, k9, [k2tog] x 2, k8. (29 sts)

Row 21: P 1 row.

Row 22: k1, [skpo] x 6, k3, [k2tog] x 6, k1. (17 sts)

Row 23-25: work 3 rows in st st.

Row 26: k1, [k2tog] x 8. (9 sts)

Cut yarn, thread end through remaining sts, pull tight to gather. Secure yarn ends from colour changes. Attach safety eyes. Sew up seam, leaving an opening. Stuff and sew closed. Make sure to put extra stuffing in the nose and cheeks.

Ears (make 2)

CO 3 sts.

Row 1: K 1 row.

Row 2: k1, m1, k1, m1, k1. (5 sts)

Row 3: K 1 row.

Row 4: k1, m1, k3, m1, k1. (7 sts)

Row 5-14: K 10 rows.

Bind off.

Finishing

If not using safety eyes, sew on button eyes or embroider eyes with black yarn. With length of yarn, embroider nose and mouth. Sew bound-off edge of ears onto head. Sew head securely to cast-on edge of body. Thread a length of yarn through left arm about 1 cm (¼") from top, thread yarn through body at shoulder position, then thread yarn through right arm. Thread yarn through body again, and then the left arm and pull tight. Repeat so yarn passes through each arm 3-4 times. Pull yarn tight so arms are secure, then fasten off yarn. Attach legs at lower edge of body in the same way as the arms.

HOODED CARDIGAN

Materials

25 g of DK weight yarn, pair of 3.75 (US size 5) knitting needles, four 10 mm buttons, 30 cm (12") narrow ribbon, tapestry needle, scrap yarn.

Measurements

19 cm (7½") around, 8 cm (3") long (not including hood)

Gauge/Tension

22 sts and 30 rows per 10 cm (4")

Back

CO 27 sts.

Row 1-4: knit 4 rows of garter st.

Row 5-15: beginning with p row, work 11 rows in st st.

Row 16: k1, k3tog tbl, k19, k3tog, k1. (23 sts)

Mark each end of row 16.

Row 17-27: work 11 rows in st st.

Row 28: bind off 4 sts, k15, bind off 4 sts.

Cut yarn. Place remaining sts on scrap yarn.

Right Front

CO 16 sts.

Row 1-4: knit 4 rows of garter st.
Row 5: p13, k3.
Row 6: K 1 row.
Row 7-15: repeat rows 5-6 x 4, then row 5 again.
Row 16: k12, k3tog, k1. (14 sts)

Mark last st of row 16.

Row 17: p11, k3.
Row 18: K 1 row.
Row 19-27: repeat rows 17-18 x 4, then row 17 again.
Row 28: k10, bind off 4 sts.

Cut yarn. Place remaining sts on scrap yarn.

Left Front

CO 16 sts.

Row 1: K 1 row.
Row 2: k14, yo, k2tog.
Row 3-4: K 2 rows of garter st.
Row 5: k3, p13.
Row 6: K 1 row.
Row 7-9: repeat rows 5-6, then row 5 again.
Row 10: k14, yo, k2tog.
Row 11-15: repeat rows 5-6 x 2, then row 5 again.
Row 16: k1, k3tog tbl, k12. (14 sts)

Mark first st of row 16.

Row 17: k3, p11.
Row 18: k12, yo, k2tog.
Row 19: k3, p11.
Row 20: K 1 row.
Row 21-25: repeat rows 19-20 x 2, then row 19 again.
Row 26: k12, yo, k2tog.
Row 27: k3, p11.
Row 28: Bind off 4 sts, k10.

Do not cut yarn. Place remaining sts on scrap yarn.

Hood

Sew fronts to back across shoulder seams. Place stitches from scrap yarn onto needle so WS is ready to knit (beginning of next row will still be attached to ball of yarn).

Row 1: k3, p7, pick up 1 st, p15, pick up 1 st, p7, k3. (37 sts)
Row 2: K 1 row.
Row 3: k3, p31, k3.

Repeat rows 2-3 until hood is 8 cm (3") long.

Next: k17, s2 as if to k2tog, k1, psso, k17. (35 sts)
Next: k3, p29, k3.
Next: k16, s2 as if to k2tog, k1, psso, k16. (33 sts)

Bind off all stitches and sew seam along hood top, or graft this seam.

Sleeves

With right side facing you, pick up 22 sts between markers on front and back.

Row 1-10: beginning with a P row, work 10 rows in st st.
Row 11-13: K 3 rows of garter st.
Row 14: bind off.

Finishing

Sew underarm and side seams. Sew buttons to right front, using buttonholes as a guide for placement. Thread ribbon around front edge of hood and knot ends.

Tip time!

A couple of tips for sewing. Gather together the cast-on stitches for the legs, arms and head before sewing the straight seams. Use mattress stitch for the straight seams and for sewing the head to the body. For the top of the bunny's feet, use a stitch called "fake grafting" or "shoulder stitch."

MISTER BUNNY
WITH A SMART SUIT

Mister Bunny

Materials

50 g of worsted weight yarn, yarn for embroidering face, two 8-10 mm black buttons or safety eyes, stuffing, pair of 4 mm (US size 6) knitting needles, tapestry needle

Measurements

20 cm (8") tall (excluding ears)

Gauge/Tension

22 sts and 32 rows per 10 cm (4")

Legs (make 2)

Begin at sole. CO 12 sts.

Row 1: P 1 row.
Row 2: k1, [m1, k1] to end. (23 sts)
Row 3: P 1 row.
Row 4: k1, [m1, k2] x 11. (34 sts)
Row 5-11: work 7 rows in st st.
Row 12: k6, [k2tog] x 5, k2, [skpo] x 5, k6. (24 sts)
Row 13: P 1 row.
Row 14: k7, bind off 10 sts, k7. (14 sts)
Row 15-17: work 3 rows in st st.
Row 18: k2, m1, k10, m1, k2. (16 sts)
Row 19-29: work 11 rows in st st.
Row 30: [k2tog] x 8.

Cut yarn, thread end through remaining sts, pull tight to gather. Sew top of foot together. Sew sole and back leg seam, leaving an opening. Stuff and sew closed.

Body

Begin at neck. CO 16 sts.

Row 1: P 1 row.
Row 2: k1, [m1, k1] to end. (31 sts)
Row 3-5: work 3 rows in st st.
Row 6: k8, m1, k15, m1, k8. (33 sts)
Row 7-13: work 7 rows in st st.
Row 14: k15, m1, k3, m1, k15. (35 sts)
Row 15-17: work 3 rows in st st.
Row 18: k3, m1, k1, m1, k27, m1, k1, m1, k3. (39 sts)
Row 19: P 1 row.
Row 20: k16, skpo, k3, k2tog, k16. (37 sts)
Row 21-23: work 3 rows in st st.
Row 24: k15, skpo, k3, k2tog, k15. (35 sts)
Row 25-27: work 3 rows in st st.
Row 28: k1, [k2tog] to end. (18 sts)
Row 29: P 1 row.
Row 30: [k2tog] x 9. (9 sts)

Cut yarn, thread end through remaining sts, pull tight to gather. Sew up back seam to neck edge (leaving cast-on edge open). Stuff body.

Right arm

Begin at paw. CO 6 sts.

Row 1: P 1 row.
Row 2: k1, [m1, k1] to end. (11 sts)
Row 3: P 1 row.
Row 4: [k2, m1] x 2, k3, [m1, k2] x 2. (15 sts)
Row 5-7: work 3 rows in st st.
Row 8: k1, [skpo] x 2, [k2tog] x 2, k6. (11 sts)
Row 9-13: work 5 rows in st st.
Row 14: k5, [m1, k3] x 2. (13 sts)
Row 15-23: work 9 rows in st st.
Row 24: k1, [k2tog] x 6. (7 sts)

Cut yarn, thread end through remaining sts, pull tight to gather. Sew up seam, leaving an opening. Stuff and sew closed.

Left Arm

Begin at paw. CO 6 sts.

Row 1: P 1 row.
Row 2: k1, [m1, k1] to end. (11 sts)
Row 3: P 1 row.
Row 4: [k2, m1] x 2, k3, [m1, k2] x 2. (15 sts)
Row 5-7: work 3 rows in st st.
Row 8: k6, [skpo] x 2, [k2tog] x 2, k1. (11 sts)
Row 9-13: work these 5 rows in st st.
Row 14: [k3, m1] x 2, k5. (13 sts)
Row 15-23: work 9 rows in st st.
Row 24: k1, [k2tog] x 6. (7 sts)

Finish same as right arm.

Head

Begin at back. CO 7 sts.

Row 1: P 1 row.
Row 2: k1, [m1, k1] to end. (13 sts)
Row 3: P 1 row.
Row 4: k1, [m1, k1] to end. (25 sts)
Row 5-7: work 3 rows in st st.
Row 8: k2, [k2, m1] x 3, k4, m1, k1, m1, k4, [m1, k2] x 3, k2. (33 sts)
Row 9-19: work 11 rows in st st.
Row 20: k7, [skpo, k1] x 2, k7, [k1, k2tog] x 2, k7. (29 sts)
Row 21: P 1 row.
Row 22: [skpo] x 7, k1, [k2tog] x 7. (15 sts)
Row 23-25: work 3 rows in st st.
Row 26: k1, [k2tog] x 7. (8 sts)

Cut yarn, thread end through remaining sts, pull tight to gather. Attach safety eyes. Sew up seam, leaving an opening. Stuff and sew closed. Make sure to put extra stuffing in the nose and cheeks.

Ears (make 2)

CO 8 sts.

Row 1-5: K 5 rows in garter st.
Row 6: k4, m1, k4. (9 sts)
Row 7-9: K 3 rows in garter st.
Row 10: k4, m1, k1, m1, k4. (11 sts)
Row 11-21: work 11 rows in garter st.
Row 22: k1, skpo, k to last st. (10 sts)
Row 23: K 1 row.
Row 24-33: repeat rows 22-23 x 5. (5 sts)
Row 34: k1, s1, k2tog, psso, k1. (3 sts)

Break off yarn. Thread end through remaining stitches, pull tight and secure yarn end.

To Make Up

If not using safety eyes, sew on button eyes, or embroider eyes with black yarn. With length of yarn, embroider nose and mouth. Fold ears in half length-wise, and sew cast-on edge to head (slanted edge of ear tips should face out). Sew head securely to cast-on edge of body. Thread a length of yarn through left arm about 1 cm (¼") from top, thread yarn through body at shoulder position, then thread yarn through right arm. Thread yarn through body again, and then the left arm and pull tight. Repeat so yarn passes through each arm 3-4 times. Pull yarn tight so arms are secure, then fasten off yarn. Attach legs at lower edge of body in the same way as the arms. If you like, make a 2.5 cm (1") diameter pom-pom for a tail and sew securely to the bunny's bum.

JACKET

Materials

20 g of sport weight yarn, pair of 3.25 mm (US size 3) knitting needles, tapestry needle, scrap yarn.

Measurements

18 cm (7") around, 8 cm (3") long

Gauge/Tension

26 sts and 34 rows per 10 cm (4")

Garter-rib pattern

Odd rows: [k1, p1] to end.
Even rows: K 1 row.

Back

CO 30 sts.

Row 1-17: work in garter-rib pattern.

Mark each end of the row 17.

Row 18: k1, k3tog tbl, k22, k3tog, k1. (26 sts)
Row 19-33: work in garter-rib pattern.
Row 34: bind off 7 sts, k12, bind off 7 sts.

Place 12 sts on scrap yarn.

Right front

CO 16 sts.

Row 1-17: work in garter-rib pattern.

Mark each end of the row 17.

Row 18: k12, k3tog, k1. (14 sts)
Row 19-33: work in garter-rib pattern.

Row 34: bind off 3 sts, k4, bind off 7 sts.
Place 4 sts on scrap yarn.

Left front

CO 16 sts.

Row 1-17: work in garter-rib pattern.
Mark each end of the row 17.

Row 18: k1, k3tog tbl, k12. (14 sts)
Row 19-33: work in garter-rib pattern.
Row 34: bind off 7 sts, k4, bind off 3 sts.
Place 4 sts on scrap yarn.

Collar

Sew front to back along shoulder seams. Place collar sts onto needle (20 sts), so that RS is ready to knit.

Row 1: k4, pick up 1, k12, pick up 1, k4. (22 sts)
Row 2-4: work 3 rows in st st.
Bind off all sts in pattern.

Sleeves

With RS of jacket facing you, pick up 24 sts between markers.

Row 1-15: work in garter-rib pattern.
Bind off all sts.

Sew together underarm and side seams, then secure all yarn ends.

WAISTCOAT

Materials

10 g of sport weight yarn, two 1 cm buttons, pair of 3.25 mm (US size 3) knitting needles, tapestry needle, scrap yarn.

Measurements

17 cm (6½") around, 6 cm (2½") long

Gauge/Tension

26 sts and 34 rows per 10 cm (4")

Back

CO 28 sts.

Row 1-4: work in garter rib pattern.
Row 5-13: beginning with a P row, work 9 rows in st st.
Row 14: s1, skpo, k to last 3 sts, k2tog, k1. (26 sts)
Row 15: s1, p to end.
Row 16-17: repeat these row 12-13 (24 sts)
Row 18-26: work 9 rows in st st, s1 at beg of all rows.
Row 27: s1, p6, bind off 10 sts, p7.
Row 28: s1, k6 (Right Front).
Place other 7 sts on scrap yarn (Left Front).

Right front

Row 29-31: work 3 rows in st st, s1 at beg of all rows.
Row 32: s1, k to last 2 sts, m1, k2. (8 sts)
Row 33: s1, p to end.
Row 34-39: repeat rows 32-33 x 3 (11 sts).
Row 40: s1, k1, m1, k7, m1, k2. (13 sts)
Row 41: s1, p12.
Row 42: s1, k1, m1, k9, m1, k2. (15 sts)
Row 43-45: work 3 rows in st st, s1 at beg of WS rows.
Row 46: k11, skpo, yo, k2.
Row 47: s1, p14.
Row 48: K 1 row.
Row 49-50: repeat rows 47-48.
Row 51: s1, p14.
Row 52: k11, skpo, yo, k2.
Row 53-55: work in garter rib pattern.
Row 56: Bind off in pattern.

Left front

Place 7 sts back onto needle, so RS is ready to knit. Attach yarn.

Row 28-31: work 4 rows in st st, s1 at beg of all rows.
Row 32: s1, k1, m1, k to end. (8 sts)
Row 33: s1, p to end.

Row 34-39: repeat rows 32-33 x 3. (11 sts)
Row 40: s1, k1, m1, k7, m1, k2. (13 sts)
Row 41: s1, p12.
Row 42: s1, k1, m1, k9, m1, k2. (15 sts)
Row 43-52: work 10 rows in st st, s1 at beg of RS rows.
Row 53-55: work in garter rib pattern.
Row 56: Bind off in pattern.

Sew together side seams, leaving openings big enough for arms. Secure yarn ends. Sew buttons to left front.

CHIPMUNK

Materials

50 g of worsted weight yarn in brown (MC), 10 g of worsted weight yarn in white (CC), 10 g of eyelash yarn to match MC (optional), black yarn for embroidery, two 8-10 mm black buttons or safety eyes, stuffing, pair of 4 mm (US size 6) knitting needles, tapestry needle.

Measurements

17 cm (7") tall

Gauge/Tension

22 sts and 32 rows per 10 cm (4")

Legs (make 2)

Begin at sole. CO 10 sts with MC.

Row 1: P 1 row.
Row 2: k1, [m1, k1] to end. (19 sts)
Row 3: P 1 row.
Row 4: k4, [m1, k3] x 5. (24 sts)
Row 5-7: work 3 rows in st st.
Row 8: k8, [skpo] x 2, [k2tog] x 2, k8. (20 sts)
Row 9: p6, [p2tog] x 2, [p2tog tbl] x 2, p6. (16 sts)
Row 10: k7, k2tog, k7. (15 sts)
Row 11-13: work 3 rows in st st.
Row 14: k2, m1, k11, m1, k2. (17 sts)
Row 15-21: work 7 rows in st st.
Row 22: k1, [k2tog] x 8. (9 sts)

Cut yarn, thread end through remaining sts, pull tight to gather. Sew sole and back leg seam, leaving an opening. Stuff and sew closed.

Body Back

Start at neck. CO 9 sts with MC.

Row 1: P 1 row.
Row 2: k1, [m1, k1] to end. (17 sts)
Row 3-7: work 5 rows in st st.
Row 8: k2, m1, k13, m1, k2. (19 sts)
Row 9-17: work 9 rows in st st.
Row 18: k6, m1, k1, m1, k5, m1, k1, m1, k6. (23 sts)
Row 18-27: work 9 rows in st st.
Row 28: k1, [k2tog] to end. (12 sts)
Row 29: P 1 row.
Row 30: k2, [k2tog] x 4, k2. (8 sts)

Bind off.

Body Front

Start at neck. CO 8 sts with CC.

Row 1: P 1 row.
Row 2: k1, [m1, k1] to end. (15 sts)
Row 3-5: work 3 rows in st st.
Row 6: k7, m1, k1, m1, k7. (17 sts)
Row 7-13: work 7 rows in st st.
Row 14: k7, m1, k3, m1, k7. (19 sts)
Row 15-19: work 5 rows in st st.
Row 20: k6, skpo, k3, k2tog, k6. (17 sts)
Row 21-23: work 3 rows in st st.
Row 24: k5, skpo, k3, k2tog, k5. (15 sts)
Row 25-27: work 3 rows in st st.
Row 28: k1, [k2tog] x 7. (8 sts)
Row 29: P 1 row.

Bind off. Sew back to front along side and bottom seams, leaving CO edge open. Stuff body.

Right arm

Begin at paw. CO 6 sts with MC.

Chipmunk
with a Cable Pullover

Row 1: P 1 row.
Row 2: k1, [m1, k1] to end. (11 sts)
Row 3: P 1 row.
Row 4: [k2, m1] x 2, k3, [m1, k2] x 2. (15 sts)
Row 5-7: work 3 rows in st st.
Row 8: k1, [skpo] x 2, [k2tog] x 2, k6. (11 sts)
Row 9-13: work 5 rows in st st.
Row 14: k5, [m1, k3] x 2. (13 sts)
Row 15-21: work 7 rows in st st.
Row 22: k1, [k2tog] x 6. (7 sts)

Cut yarn, thread end through remaining sts, pull tight to gather. Sew up seam, leaving an opening. Stuff and sew closed.

Left arm

Begin at paw. CO 6 sts with MC.

Row 1: P 1 row.
Row 2: k1, [m1, k1] to end. (11 sts)
Row 3: P 1 row.
Row 4: [k2, m1] x 2, k3, [m1, k2] x 2. (15 sts)
Row 5-7: work 3 rows in st st.
Row 8: k6, [skpo] x 2, [k2tog] x 2, k1. (11 sts)
Row 9-13: work 5 rows in st st.
Row 14: [k3, m1] x 2, k5. (13 sts)
Row 15-21: work 7 rows in st st.
Row 22: k1, [k2tog] x 6. (7 sts)

Finish same as right arm.

Head

Begin at back. CO 7 sts with MC.

Row 1: P 1 row.
Row 2: k1, [m1, k1] to end. (13 sts)
Row 3: P 1 row.
Row 4: k1, [m1, k1] to end. (25 sts)
Row 5-9: work 5 rows in st st.
Row 10: k3, [k1, m1] x 4, k11, [m1, k1] x 4, k3. (33 sts)
Row 11-19: work 9 rows in st st.
Row 20: k3, [k2tog, k1] x 3, k9, [k1, ssk] x 3, k3. (27 sts)
Row 21: P 1 row.
Row 22: k1, [k2tog, k2] x 3, k1, [k2, ssk] x 3, k1. (21 sts)
Row 23: P 1 row.
Row 24: k1, [k2tog, k2] x 2, k3, [k2, ssk] x 2, k1. (17 sts)
Row 25: P 1 row.
Row 26: k1, [k2tog, k1] x 2, k3, [k1, ssk] x 2, k1. (13 sts)
Row 27: P 1 row.
Row 28: k1, [k2tog] x 2, k3, [ssk] x 2, k1. (9 sts)

Cut yarn, thread end through remaining sts, pull tight to gather. Attach safety eyes. Sew up seam, leaving an opening. Stuff and sew closed. Make sure to put extra stuffing in the nose and cheeks.

Ears (make 2)

CO 6 sts with MC.

Row 1-3: K 3 rows in garter st.
Row 4: k1, skpo, k2tog, k1. (4 sts)
Row 5: K 1 row.
Row 6: k1, skpo, k1. (3 sts)

Cut yarn, thread end though sts, pull tight to gather. Secure yarn end.

Tail

CO 8 sts with MC or eyelash yarn.

Row 1: P 1 row.
Row 2: k2, [m1, k1] x 6. (14 sts)

Work in st st until tail is 8 cm (3") long or desired length.

Next: k1, [k1, k2tog] x 4, k1. (10 sts)
Next: P 1 row.
Next: k1, [k2tog] x 4, k1. (6 sts)

Cut yarn, thread end through remaining sts, pull tight to gather. Sew seam, adding a small amount of stuffing as you sew.

Finishing

If not using safety eyes, sew on button eyes, or embroider eyes with black yarn. With black yarn, embroider nose and mouth. Sew cst-on edge of ears in place on head. Sew head securely to cast-on edge of body. Using duplicate stitch method, embroider lines on face and back with white and black yarn. Thread a length of yarn through left arm about 1 cm (¼") from top, thread yarn through body at shoulder position, then thread yarn through right arm. Thread yarn through body again, and then the left arm and pull tight. Repeat so yarn passes through each arm 3-4 times. Pull yarn tight so arms are secure, then fasten off yarn. Attach legs at lower edge of body in the same way as the arms. Sew tail to chipmunk's bum.

CABLE PULLOVER

Materials

25 g of worsted weight yarn, pair of 4 mm (US size 6) knitting needles, darning needle, scrap yarn, length of matching cord (optional).

Measurements

17 cm (7") tall

Gauge/Tension

22 sts and 32 rows per 10 cm (4")

Front

CO 24 sts.

Row 1: [k1, p1] to end.
Row 2: [p1, k1] to end.
Row 3-4: repeat rows 1-2.
Row 5: k4, p5, [p1, k1] x 3, p5, k4.
Row 6: p4, c1f, k1, c1b, [k1, p1] x 3, c1f, k1, c1b, p4.
Row 7-13: repeat rows 5-6 three times, then row 5.
Row 14: p1, p3tog, c1f, k1, c1b, [k1, p1] x 3, c1f, k1, c1b, p3tog, p1. (20 sts)

Mark each end of row 14.

Row 15: k2, p5, [p1, k1] x 3, p5, k2.
Row 16: p2, c1f, k1, c1b, k1, p1, k1. (Left Front)

Place remaining 10 sts on scrap yarn (Right Front).

Left Front

Row 17: k1, p1, k1, p5, k2.
Row 18: p2, c1f, k1, c1b, k1, p1, k1.
Row 19-27: repeat rows 17-18 x 4, then row 17 again.
Row 28: bind off 4 sts, [p1, k1] x 3. (6 sts)

Place 6 sts on scrap yarn.

Right front

Place 10 sts from scrap yarn onto needle so RS is ready to knit.

Row 16: p1, k1, p1, c1f, k1, c1b, p2.
Row 17: k2, p5, p1, k1, p1.
Row 18-27: repeat rows 16-17 x 5.
Row 28: [k1, p1] x 3, bind off 4 sts. (6 sts)

Place 6 sts on scrap yarn.

Back

CO 24 sts.

Row 1: [k1, p1] to end.
Row 2: [p1, k1] to end.
Row 3-4: repeat rows 1-2.
Row 5-13: starting with K row, work 9 rows in st st.
Row 14: p1, p3tog, p16, p3tog, p1. (20 sts)

Mark each end of row 14.

Row 15-27: work 13 rows in st st.
Row 28: bind off 4 sts, [k1, p1] x 6, bind off 4 sts. (12 sts)

Place remaining sts on scrap yarn. Sew front to back along shoulder seams (back of pullover is reverse stockinette, so purl side is RS).

Collar

Place sts from front and back onto needle so RS is ready to knit. (24 sts)

Row 1: [k1, p1] to end.
Row 2: [p1, k1] to end.
Row 3-8: repeat rows 1-2 x 3.

Bind off in pattern. Secure all yarn ends.

Sleeves

With RS facing you, pick up 19 sts between markers on front and back.

Row 1: k7, p5, k7.

Row 2: p7, c1f, k1, c1b, p7.
Row 3-8: repeat rows 1-2 x 3.
Row 9: k1, [p1, k1] to end.
Row 10: repeat row 9.

Bind off in pattern. Sew side and underarm seams. Blocking will help straighten pullover, and make it look better. Optional: lace open front of pullover with cord.

SIAMESE KITTY

Materials
25 g of dark brown (DB) worsted weight yarn, 25 g of cream (C) worsted weight yarn, 10 g of medium brown (MB) worsted weight yarn, black yarn for embroidery, two 8-10 mm blue buttons or safety eyes, stuffing, pair of 4 mm (US size 6) knitting needles, tapestry needle

Measurements
approx. 20cm (8") tall

Gauge/Tension
22 sts and 32 rows per 10 cm (4")

Legs (make 2)
Begin at sole. CO 10 sts with DB.

Row 1: P 1 row.
Row 2: k1, [m1, k1] to end. (19 sts)
Row 3: P 1 row.
Row 4: k4, [m1, k3] x 5. (24 sts)
Row 5-7: work 3 rows in st st.
Row 8: k8, [skpo] x 2, [k2tog] x 2, k8. (20 sts)
Row 9: p6, [p2tog] x 2, [p2tog tbl] x 2, p6. (16 sts)
Row 10: k7, k2tog, k7. (15 sts)
Row 11-13: work 3 rows in st st.
Row 14: k2, m1, k11, m1, k2. (17 sts)

Break off DB and start next row with MB

Row 15-17: work 3 rows in st st.

Break off MB and start next row with C.

Row 18-25: work 8 rows in st st.
Row 26: k1, [k2tog] x 8. (9 sts)

Cut yarn, thread end through remaining sts, pull tight to gather. Sew sole and back leg seam, leaving an opening. Stuff and sew closed.

Body
Begin at neck. CO 16 sts with C.

Row 1: P 1 row.
Row 2: k1, [m1, k1] to end. (31 sts)
Row 3-5: work 3 rows in st st.
Row 6: k8, m1, k15, m1, k8. (33 sts)
Row 7-13: work 7 rows in st st.
Row 14: k15, m1, k3, m1, k15. (35 sts)
Row 15-17: work 3 rows in st st.
Row 18: k3, m1, k1, m1, k27, m1, k1, m1, k3. (39 sts)
Row 19: P 1 row.
Row 20: k16, skpo, k3, k2tog, k16. (37 sts)
Row 21-23: work 3 rows in st st.
Row 24: k15, skpo, k3, k2tog, k15. (35 sts)
Row 25-27: work 3 rows in st st.
Row 28: k1, [k2tog] to end. (18 sts)
Row 29: P 1 row.
Row 30: [k2tog] x 9. (9 sts)

Cut yarn, thread end through remaining sts, pull tight to gather. Sew up back seam to neck edge (leaving cast-on edge open). Stuff body.

Right arm
Begin at paw. CO 6 sts with DB.

Row 1: P 1 row.
Row 2: k1, [m1, k1] to end. (11 sts)
Row 3: P 1 row.
Row 4: [k2, m1] x 2, k3, [m1, k2] x 2. (15 sts)
Row 5-7: work 3 rows in st st.
Row 8: k1, [skpo] x 2, [k2tog] x 2, k6. (11 sts)
Row 9-12: work 4 rows in st st.

25

Siamese Kitty
WITH A SWEETHEART DRESS

Break off DB and start next row with MB.

Row 13: P 1 row.
Row 14: k5, [m1, k3] x 2. (13 sts)
Row 15: P 1 row.

Break off MB and start next row with C.

Row 16-23: work 8 rows in st st.
Row 24: k1, [k2tog] 6 times. (7 sts)

Cut yarn, thread end through remaining sts, pull tight to gather. Sew up seam, leaving an opening. Stuff and sew closed.

Left arm

Begin at paw. CO 6 sts with DB.

Row 1: P 1 row.
Row 2: k1, [m1, k1] to end. (11 sts)
Row 3: P 1 row.
Row 4: [k2, m1] x 2, k3, [m1, k2] x 2. (15 sts)
Row 5-7: work 3 rows in st st.
Row 8: k6, [skpo] x 2, [k2tog] x 2, k1. (11 sts)
Row 9-12: work 4 rows in st st.

Break off DB and start next row with MB.

Row 13: P 1 row.
Row 14: k3, m1, k3, m1, k5. (13 sts)
Row 15: P 1 row.

Break off MB and start next row with C.

Row 16-23: work 8 rows in st st.
Row 24: k1, [k2tog] 6 times. (7 sts)

Finish same as right arm.

Head

Begin at back. CO 7 sts with C.

Row 1: P 1 row.
Row 2: k1, [m1, k1] to end. (13 sts)
Row 3: P 1 row.
Row 4: k1, [m1, k1] to end. (25 sts)
Row 5-7: work 3 rows in st st.
Row 8: [k2, m1] x 4, k9, [m1, k2] x 4. (33 sts)
Row 9-15: work 7 rows in st st.

Break off C and start next row with MB.

Row 16-18: work 3 rows in st st.

Break off MB and start next row with DB.

Row 19: P 1 row.
Row 20: k7, [skpo, k1] x 2, k7, [k1, k2tog] x 2, k7. (29 sts)
Row 21: P 1 row.
Row 22: k1, [skpo] x 6, k3, [k2tog] x 6, k1. (17 sts)
Row 23-25: work 3 rows in st st.
Row 26: k1, [k2tog] to end. (9 sts)

Break off yarn. Thread end through remaining stitches and pull tight to gather. Attach safety eyes to head. Sew up seam, leaving an opening. Stuff and close opening. Make sure to put a bit of extra stuffing in the nose and cheeks.

Ears (make 2)

CO 9 sts.

Row 1: K 1 row.
Row 2: k1, skpo, k to end. (8 sts)
Row 3: K 1 row.
Row 4-9: Repeat rows 2-3 x 3. (5 sts)
Row 10: k1, [skpo] x 2. (3 sts)
Row 11: K 1 row.

Break off yarn. Thread end through remaining stitches, pull tight and secure end.

Tail

CO 10 sts with DB.

Beginning with P row, work in st st until tail is about 12 cm (5") long.

Break off yarn. Thread end through stitches and pull tight to gather. Sew up seam, adding small amount of stuffing as you sew.

Finishing

Sew on button eyes, or embroider with yarn. Using black yarn, embroider nose and mouth. Sew cast-on edge of ears to head. Sew head securely to open neck edge of body. Thread a length of yarn through left arm about 1 cm (¼") from top, thread yarn through body at shoulder position, then thread yarn through right arm. Thread yarn through body again, and then the left arm and pull tight. Repeat so yarn passes through each arm 3-4 times. Pull yarn tight so arms are secure, then fasten off yarn. Attach legs at lower edge of body in the same way as the arms. Sew tail to kitty's bum.

SWEETHEART DRESS

Materials

15 g of fingering weight yarn, pair of 2.75 mm and 3.25 mm (US size 2 and 3) knitting needles, tapestry needle, small button (optional)

Measurements

9 cm (3½") long, 25 cm (10") around

Gauge

28 sts and 44 rows per 10 cm (4")

Skirt

With 3.25 mm needles, CO 66 sts.

Row 1-3: K 3 rows in garter st.
Row 4: k3, [yo, skpo, k4] x 10, k3.
Row 5: k3, p60, k3.
Row 6: k3, [k1, yo, skpo, k1, k2tog, yo] x 10, k3.
Row 7: k3, p60, k3.
Row 8: k3, [k2, yo, s1, k2tog, psso, yo, k1] x 10, k3.
Row 9: k3, p60, k3.
Row 10-21: repeat rows 4-9 x 2.
Row 22: K 1 row.
Row 23: k3, p60, k3.

Change to 2.75 mm needles on next row.

Row 24: k3, [k1, k2tog, k1] x 15, k1, k2tog. (50 sts)
Row 25: k20, p10, k20.
Row 26: K 1 row.
Row 27: k20, p10, k20.
Row 28: Bind off 17 sts, k16, bind off 17 sts. (16 sts)

Break off yarn, and attach to remaining sts on needle.

Bib

Row 29: k3, p10, k3.
Row 30: K 1 row.
Row 31-32: repeat rows 29-30.
Row 33: k3, p4, k2, p4, k3.
Row 34: K 1 row.
Row 35: k3, p3, k4, p3, k3.
Row 36: k4, k2tog, k2, place other 8 sts on holder.

Continue on 7 sts still on needle for left strap.

Left Strap

Row 37: k3, p1, k3.
Row 38: k3, k2tog, k2. (6 sts)
Row 39: K 1 row.
Row 40: k2, k2tog, k2. (5 sts)
Row 41: K 1 row.
Row 42: [k2tog] x 2, k1. (3 sts)

K in garter st until strap is 5 cm (2") long from last decrease row, then bind off.

Right Strap

Place remaining 8 sts on needle, so RS is ready to knit.

Row 36: k2, skpo, k4.
Row 37: k3, p1, k3.
Row 38: k2, skpo, k3. (6 sts)
Row 39: K 1 row.
Row 40: k2, skpo, k2. (5 sts)
Row 41: K 1 row.
Row 42: k1, [skpo] x 2. (3 sts)

K in garter st until strap is 5 cm long from last decrease row, then bind off.

Finishing

Secure yarn ends. Cross straps in back, and sew ends to waistband about 1 cm (⅜") from center back. Sew together waistband at center back, or make a button loop and attach a button.

Tiger
IN A SUMMER DRESS

TIGER

Materials

25 g of orange worsted weight yarn (OR), 25 g of black worsted weight yarn (BL), 10 g of white worsted weight yarn (WH), pink yarn for embroidering face, two 8-10 mm buttons or safety eyes, stuffing, pair of 4 mm (US size 6) knitting needles, tapestry needle

Measurements

Approx. 20 cm (8") tall

Gauge/Tension

22 sts and 32 rows per 10 cm (4")

Legs (make 2)

Begin at sole. CO 10 sts with WH.

Row 1: P 1 row.
Row 2: k1, [m1, k1] to end. (19 sts)
Row 3: P 1 row.
Row 4: k4, [m1, k3] x 5. (24 sts)

Break off WH, then alternate 2 rows OR and 2 rows BL.

Row 5-7: work 3 rows in st st.
Row 8: k8, [skpo] x 2, [k2tog] x 2, k8. (20 sts)
Row 9: p6, [p2tog] x 2, [p2tog tbl] x 2, p6. (16 sts)
Row 10: k7, k2tog, k7. (15 sts)
Row 11-13: work 3 rows in st st.
Row 14: k2, m1, k11, m1, k2. (17 sts)
Row 15-25: work 11 rows in st st.
Row 26: k1, [k2tog] x 8. (9 sts)

Cut yarn, thread end through remaining sts, pull tight to gather. Sew up sole and back leg seam, leaving an opening. Stuff and sew closed.

Body

Begin at neck. CO 16 sts with WH.

Row 1: P 1 row.
Row 2: k1, [m1, k1] to end. (31 sts)

Break off WH, then alternate 2 rows OR and 2 rows BL.

Row 3-5: work 3 rows in st st.
Row 6: k8, m1, k15, m1, k8. (33 sts)
Row 7-13: work 7 rows in st st.
Row 14: k15, m1, k3, m1, k15. (35 sts)
Row 15-17: work 3 rows in st st.
Row 18: k3, m1, k1, m1, k27, m1, k1, m1, k3. (39 sts)
Row 19: P 1 row.
Row 20: k16, skpo, k3, k2tog, k16. (37 sts)
Row 21-23: work 3 rows in st st.
Row 24: k15, skpo, k3, k2tog, k15. (35 sts)
Row 25-27: work 3 rows in st st.
Row 28: k1, [k2tog] to end. (18 sts)
Row 29: P 1 row.
Row 30: [k2tog] x 9. (9 sts)

Cut yarn, thread end through remaining sts, pull tight to gather. Sew up back seam to neck edge (leaving cast-on edge open). Stuff body.

Right arm

Begin at paw. CO 6 sts with WH.

Row 1: P 1 row.
Row 2: k1, [m1, k1] to end. (11 sts)
Row 3: P 1 row.
Row 4: [k2, m1] x 2, k3, [m1, k2] x 2. (15 sts)

Break off WH, then alternate 2 rows OR and 2 rows BL.

Row 5-7: work 3 rows in st st.
Row 8: k1, [skpo] x 2, [k2tog] x 2, k6. (11 sts)
Row 9-13: work 5 rows in st st.
Row 14: k5, [m1, k3] x 2. (13 sts)
Row 15-23: work 9 rows in st st.
Row 24: k1, [k2tog] x 6. (7 sts)

Cut yarn, thread end through remaining sts, pull tight to gather. Sew up seam, leaving an opening. Stuff and sew closed.

Left arm

Begin at paw. CO 6 sts with WH.

Row 1: P 1 row.
Row 2: k1, [m1, k1] to end. (11 sts)
Row 3: P 1 row.
Row 4: [k2, m1] x 2, k3, [m1, k2] x 2. (15 sts)

Break off WH, then alternate 2 rows OR and 2 rows BL.

Row 5-7: work 3 rows in st st.
Row 8: k6, [skpo] x 2, [k2tog] x 2, k1. (11 sts)
Row 9-13: work 5 rows in st st.
Row 14: [k3, m1] x 2, k5. (13 sts)
Row 15-23: work 9 rows in st st.
Row 24: k1, [k2tog] x 6. (7 sts)

Finish same as right arm.

Head

Begin at back. CO 7 sts with OR. Alternate 2 rows OR and 2 rows BL until row 18.

Row 1: P 1 row.
Row 2: k1, [m1, k1] to end. (13 sts)
Row 3: P 1 row.
Row 4: k1, [m1, k1] to end. (25 sts)
Row 5-7: work 3 rows in st st.
Row 8: [k2, m1] x 4, k9, [m1, k2] x 4. (33 sts)
Row 9-18: work 10 rows in st st.
Row 19: OR P 1 row.
Row 20: WH k8, [skpo] x 2, OR k9, WH [k2tog] x 2, k8. (29 sts)
Row 21: WH p11, OR p7, WH p11.
Row 22: WH k1, [skpo] x 5, OR skpo, k3, k2tog, WH [k2tog] x 5, k1. (17 sts)
Row 23: WH p6, OR p5, WH p6.
Row 24: WH k6, OR k5, WH k6.
Row 25: WH p6, OR p5, WH p6.
Row 26: WH k1, [k2tog] x 8. (9 sts)

Cut yarn, thread end through remaining sts, pull tight to gather. Secure yarn ends from colour changes. Attach safety eyes. Sew up seam, leaving an opening. Stuff and sew closed. Make sure to put extra stuffing in the nose and cheeks.

Ears (make 2)

CO 3 sts with BL.

Row 1: P 1 row.
Row 2: k1, [m1, k1] x 2. (5 sts)
Row 3: P 1 row.
Row 4: k1, [m1, k1] x 4. (9 sts)
Row 5-6: P 2 rows.

Break off BL and start next row with WH.

Row 7: P 1 row.
Row 8: [skpo] x 2, k1, [k2tog] x 2. (5 sts)
Row 9: P 1 row.
Row 10: skpo, k1, k2tog. (3 sts)

Cut yarn, thread end through remaining stitches, pull tight to gather. Fold ear in half, with white to front and black to back.

Tail

CO 10 sts with BL.

Row 1-32: work in st st, alternating 2 rows BL and 2 rows OR.

Break off OR and start next row with WH.

Row 33-36: work 4 rows in st st.

Cut yarn, thread end through remaining sts, pull tight to gather. Sew seam, adding a small amount of stuffing as you sew.

Finishing

If not using safety eyes, sew on button eyes, or embroider eyes with black yarn. With length of yarn, embroider nose and mouth. Sew ears in place on head (purl ridge is upper ear edge). Sew head securely to cast-on edge of body. Thread a length of yarn through left arm about 1 cm (¼") from top, thread yarn through body at shoulder position, then thread yarn through right arm. Thread yarn through body again, and then the left arm and pull tight. Repeat so yarn passes through each arm 3-4 times. Pull yarn tight so arms are secure, then fasten off yarn. Attach legs at lower edge of body in the same way as the arms. Sew tail to tiger's bum.

Summer Dress

Materials

25 g of sport weight yarn in main colour (MC), 10 g of sport weight yarn in contrasting colour (CC), 3 mm and 3.25 mm needles (US sizes 2.5 & 3, sets of dpns or long circular needles for magic loop method), tapestry needle, stitch markers, scrap yarn

Measurements

11.5 cm (4½") long

Tension/Gauge

28 sts and 36 rows to 10 cm (4") in st st on 3.25 mm needles.

Skirt

CO 48 sts with MC yarn onto 3.25 mm needles. Distribute stitches evenly, depending on method selected (dpns or circular).

Row 1: join in round, P 1 row.
Row 2: K 1 row.
Row 3: [k2, m1, k1, m1] x 16. (80 sts)
Row 4-5: work 2 rows in st st.
Row 6-25: work pattern chart twice. Each chart row repeats x 8 per round. Use stitch markers to mark each repeat.
Row 26-28: work 3 rows in st st.

Switch to 3 mm needles on next row.

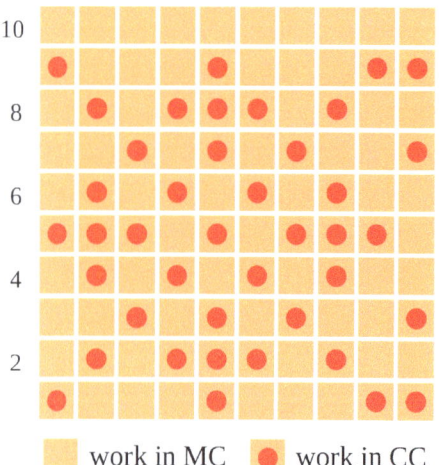

Row 29: [k2tog] x 40 in CC. (40 sts)
Row 30: K 1 row in CC.
Row 31: K 1 row in MC.

Work rest of dress in MC on 3 mm needles.

Left Front

Row 32: k11.

Place 9 sts on scrap yarn (Right Front). Place other 20 sts on scrap yarn (Back). Fronts and Back are worked flat.

Row 33: k2, p9.
Row 34: k1, skpo, k8. (10 sts)
Row 35: k2, p8.
Row 36: k6, k2tog, k2. (9 sts)
Row 37: k2, p7.
Row 38: k5, k2tog, k2. (8 sts)
Row 39: k2, p6.
Row 40: k4, k2tog, k2. (7 sts)
Row 41: k2, p5.
Row 42: k3, k2tog, k2. (6 sts)
Row 43: k2, p4.
Row 44: k2, k2tog, k1. (5 sts)
Row 45: k2, p3.
Row 46: place 5 sts on scrap yarn, or bind off 5 sts.

Right Front

Place 9 sts back onto needle so RS is ready to knit.

Row 32: pick up 2 sts on WS of garter stitch edge, k9. (11 sts)
Row 33: p9, k2.
Row 34: k8, k2tog, k1. (10 sts)
Row 35: p8, k2.
Row 36: k2, skpo, k6. (9 sts)
Row 37: p7, k2.
Row 38: k2, skpo, k5. (8 sts)
Row 39: p6, k2.
Row 40: k2, skpo, k4. (7 sts)
Row 41: p5, k2.
Row 42: k2, skpo, k3. (6 sts)
Row 43: p4, k2.
Row 44: k2, skpo, k2. (5 sts)
Row 45: p3, k2.
Row 46: place 5 sts on scrap yarn, or bind off 5 sts.

Back

Place 20 sts onto needle so RS is ready to knit.

Row 32-33: work 2 rows in st st.
Row 34: k1, skpo, k14, k2tog, k1. (18 sts)
Row 35-43: work 9 rows in st st.
Row 45: k5, bind off 8, k5. Or, bind off all sts.

Graft or sew shoulder seams. Secure all yarn ends.

MOUSE

Materials

40 g of worsted weight yarn in main colour (MC), 15 g of worsted weight yarn in contrasting colour (CC), yarn for embroidering face, two 8-10 mm black buttons or safety eyes, stuffing, pair of 4 mm (US size 6) knitting needles, two 4 mm dpns (optional), tapestry needle.

Measurements

Approx. 18 cm (7") tall.

Gauge/Tension

22 sts and 32 rows to 10 cm (4") in st st.

Legs (make 2)

Begin at sole. CO 10 sts with MC.

Row 1: P 1 row.
Row 2: k1, [m1, k1] to end. (19 sts)
Row 3: P 1 row.
Row 4: k4, [m1, k3] x 5. (24 sts)
Row 5-7: work 3 rows in st st.
Row 8: k8, [skpo] x 2, [k2tog] x 2, k8. (20 sts)
Row 9: p6, [p2tog] x 2, [p2tog tbl] x 2, p6. (16 sts)
Row 10: k7, k2tog, k7. (15 sts)
Row 11-13: work 3 rows in st st.
Row 14: k2, m1, k11, m1, k2. (17 sts)
Row 15-21: work 7 rows in st st.
Row 22: k1, [k2tog] x 8. (9 sts)

Cut yarn, thread end through remaining sts, pull tight to gather. Sew sole and back leg seam, leaving an opening. Stuff and sew closed.

Body

Begin at neck. CO 16 sts with MC.

Row 1: P 1 row.
Row 2: k1, [m1,k1] to end. (31 sts)
Row 3-5: work 3 rows in st st.
Row 6: k8, m1, k15, k8. (33 sts)
Row 7-13: work 7 rows in st st.
Row 14: k15, m1, k3, m1, k15. (35 sts)
Row 15-17: work 3 rows in st st.
Row 18: k3, m1, k1, m1, k27, m1, k1, m1, k3. (39 sts)
Row 19: P 1 row.
Row 20: k16, skpo, k3, k2tog, k16. (37 sts)
Row 21-23: work 3 rows in st st.
Row 24: k15, skpo, k3, k2tog, k15. (35 sts)
Row 25-27: work 3 rows in st st.
Row 28: K1, [k2tog] to end. (18 sts)
Row 29: P 1 row.
Row 30: [k2tog] x 9. (9 sts)

Cut yarn, thread end through remaining sts, pull tight to gather. Sew up back seam to neck edge (leaving cast-on edge open). Stuff body.

Right arm

Begin at paw. CO 6 sts with MC.

Row 1: P 1 row.
Row 2: k1, [m1, k1] to end. (11 sts)
Row 3: P 1 row.
Row 4: [k2, m1] x 2, k3, [m1, k2] x 2. (15 sts)
Row 5-7: work 3 rows in st st.
Row 8: k1, [skpo] x 2, [k2tog] x 2, k6. (11 sts)
Row 9-13: work 5 rows in st st.

33

MOUSE
WITH A RAGLAN PULLOVER

Row 14: k5, [m1, k3] x 2. (13 sts)
Row 15-21: work 7 rows in st st.
Row 22: k1, [k2tog] x 6. (7 sts)

Cut yarn, thread end through remaining sts, pull tight to gather. Sew up seam, leaving an opening. Stuff and sew closed.

Left arm

Begin at paw. CO 6 sts with MC.

Row 1: P 1 row.
Row 2: k1, [m1, k1] to end.
Row 3: P 1 row.
Row 4: [k2, m1] x 2, k3, [m1, k2] x 2. (15 sts)
Row 5-7: work 3 rows in st st.
Row 8: k6, [skpo] x 2, [k2tog] x 2, k1. (11 sts)
Row 9-13: work 5 rows in st st.
Row 14: [k3, m1] x 2, k5. (13 sts)
Row 15-21: work 7 rows in st st.
Row 22: k1, [k2tog] x 6. (7 sts)

Finish same as right arm.

Head

The intarsia section is marked with the yarn colour for each set of sts. Begin at back. CO 7 sts with MC.

Row 1: P 1 row.
Row 2: k1, [m1, k1] to end. (13 sts)
Row 3: P 1 row.
Row 4: k1, [m1, k1] to end. (25 sts)
Row 5-9: work 5 rows in st st.
Row 10: k3, [k1, m1] x 4, k11, [m1, k1] x 4, k3. (33 sts)
Row 11-19: work 9 rows in st st.
Row 20: k3, [k2tog, k1] x 3, k9, [k1, ssk] x 3, k3. (27 sts)
Row 21: CC p7, MC p13, CC p7.
Row 22: CC k1, k2tog, k4, k2tog, MC k9, CC ssk, k4, ssk, k1. (23 sts)
Row 23: CC p7, MC p9, CC p7.
Row 24: CC k1, k2tog, k2, k2tog, MC k9, CC ssk, k2, ssk, k1. (19 sts)
Row 25: CC p5, MC p9, CC p5.
Row 26: CC k1, [k2tog] x 2, MC k9, CC [ssk] x 2, k1. (15 sts)
Row 27: CC p3, MC p9, CC p3.
Row 28: CC k3, MC [k2tog] x 2, k1, [ssk] x 2, CC k3. (11 sts)
Row 29: CC p3, MC p5, CC p3.
Row 30: CC k1, [k2tog] x 2, k1, [ssk] x 2, k1. (9 sts)

Cut yarn, thread end through remaining sts, pull tight to gather. Secure yarn ends from colour changes. Attach safety eyes. Sew up seam, leaving an opening. Stuff and sew closed. Make sure to put extra stuffing in the nose and cheeks.

Ears (make 2)

CO 3 sts with MC.

Row 1: P 1 row.
Row 2: k1, [m1, k1] x 2. (5 sts)
Row 3: P 1 row.
Row 4: k1, [m1, k1] x 4. (9 sts)
Row 5: P 1 row.
Row 6: k3, [m1, k1] x 4, k2. (13 sts)
Row 7-8: work 2 rows in st st.
Row 9: K 1 row.

Switch to CC on next row.

Row 10-11: work 2 rows in st st.
Row 12: k2, [skpo] x 2, k1, [k2tog] x 2, k2. (9 sts)
Row 13: P 1 row.
Row 14: [skpo] x 2, k1, [k2tog] x 2. (5 sts)
Row 15: P 1 row.
Row 16: skpo, k1, k2tog. (3 sts)

Cut yarn, thread end through remaining stitches, pull tight to gather. Fold ear in half, with CC to front and MC to back.

Tail

Work 13 cm (5") of 4 st I-cord on dpns.

Cut yarn, thread end through remaining sts, then secure yarn end. Or, braid strands of yarn together.

To Make Up

If not using safety eyes, sew on button eyes, or embroider eyes with black yarn. With length of yarn, embroider nose and mouth. Sew ears in place on head (purl ridge is upper ear edge). Sew head securely to cast-on edge of body. Thread a length of yarn through left arm about 1 cm (¼") from top, thread yarn through body at shoulder position, then thread yarn through right arm. Thread yarn through body again, and then the left arm and pull tight. Repeat so yarn passes through each arm 3-4 times. Pull yarn tight so arms are secure, then fasten off yarn. Attach legs at lower edge of body in the same way as the arms. Sew tail to mouse's bum.

RAGLAN PULLOVER

Materials

20 g of fingering or sport weight yarn, pair of 3.25 mm (US size 3) knitting needles, tapestry needle, scrap yarn, crochet hook and button (optional)

Measurements

19 cm (7½") around, 7.5 cm (3") long

Gauge/Tension

28 sts and 40 rows per 10 cm (4")

Front and Back

CO 30 sts.

Row 1-3: [k1, p1] to end.
Row 4-15: beginning with a k row, work 12 rows in st st.
Row 16: k1, skpo, k to last 3 sts, k2tog, k1. (28 sts)
Row 17: P 1 row.
Row 18-27: repeat rows 16-17 x 10. (18 sts)
Row 28: [k1, skpo] x 3, [k2tog, k1] x 3. (12 sts)
Row 29: p2tog, p8, p2tog tbl. (10 sts)

Cut yarn, and place sts on scrap yarn.

Pocket

CO 18 sts.

Row 1-5: beginning with a P row, work 5 rows in st st.
Row 6: s1, skpo, k to last 3 sts, k2tog, k1. (16 sts)
Row 7: s1, p to end.
Row 8-13: repeat rows 6-7 x 3. (10 sts)

Bind off. Sew pocket to front of pullover, lining up bottom edge of pocket to top edge of ribbing (to center pocket, fold front and pocket in half, mark center of each with straight pin, then match up and pin in place).

Sleeves (make 2)

CO 22 sts.

Row 1-3: [k1, p1] to end.
Row 4-11: beginning with a P row, work 8 rows in st st (or 12 rows for longer sleeves to fit other toys).
Row 12: k1, skpo, k to last 3 sts, k2tog, k1. (20 sts)
Row 13: P 1 row.
Row 14-23: repeat rows 12-13 x 10. (10 sts)
Row 24: k1, [skpo] x 2, [k2tog] x 2, k1. (6 sts)
Row 25: p2tog, p2, p2tog tbl. (4 sts)

Cut yarn, and place sts on scrap yarn. Sew sleeves to front and back along decreased edges, leaving one shoulder seam open.

Collar

Place all 28 sts from scrap yarn onto needle so RS is ready to knit.

Work 2 rows in k1, p1 ribbing.

Bind off loosely in rib.

Crochet a small button loop on collar, or sew closed along with last shoulder seam. Sew underarm and side seams.

Panda

Materials
35 g of worsted weight yarn in main colour (MC), 25 g of worsted weight yarn in white (CC), yarn for embroidering face, two 8-10 mm black buttons or safety eyes, stuffing, pair of 4 mm (US size 6) knitting needles, tapestry needle

Measurements
Approx. 20 cm (8") tall

Gauge/Tension
22 sts and 32 rows per 10 cm (4")

Legs (make 2)
Begin at sole. CO 10 sts with MC.

Row 1: P 1 row.
Row 2: k1, [m1, k1] to end. (19 sts)
Row 3: P 1 row.
Row 4: k4, [m1, k3] x 5. (24 sts)
Row 5-7: work 3 rows in st st.
Row 8: k8, [skpo] x 2, [k2tog] x 2, k8. (20 sts)
Row 9: p6, [p2tog] x 2, [p2tog tbl] x 2, p6. (16 sts)
Row 10: k7, k2tog, k7. (15 sts)
Row 11-13: work 3 rows in st st.
Row 14: k2, m1, k11, m1, k2. (17 sts)
Row 15-25: work 11 rows in st st.
Row 26: k1, [k2tog] x 8. (9 sts)

Cut yarn, thread end through remaining sts, pull tight to gather. Sew sole and back leg seam, leaving an opening. Stuff and sew closed.

Body
Begin at neck. CO 16 sts with MC.

Row 1: P 1 row.
Row 2: k1, [m1, k1] to end. (31 sts)
Row 3-5: work 3 rows in st st.
Row 6: k8, m1, k15, m1, k8. (33 sts)
Row 7-8: work 2 rows in st st.

Break off MC and start next row with CC.

Row 9-13: work 5 rows in st st.
Row 14: k15, m1, k3, m1, k15. (35 sts)
Row 15-17: work 3 rows in st st.
Row 18: k3, m1, k1, m1, k27, m1, k1, m1, k3. (39 sts)
Row 19: P 1 row.
Row 20: k16, skpo, k3, k2tog, k16. (37 sts)
Row 21-23: work 3 rows in st st.
Row 24: k15, skpo, k3, k2tog, k15. (35 sts)
Row 25-27: work 3 rows in st st.
Row 28: k1, [k2tog] to end. (18 sts)
Row 29: P 1 row.
Row 30: [k2tog] x 9. (9 sts)

Cut yarn, thread end through remaining sts, pull tight to gather. Sew up back seam to neck edge (leaving cast-on edge open). Stuff body.

Right arm
Begin at paw. CO 6 sts with MC.

Row 1: P 1 row.
Row 2: k1, [m1, k1] to end. (11 sts)
Row 3: P 1 row.
Row 4: [k2, m1] x 2, k3, [m1, k2] x 2. (15 sts)
Row 5-7: work 3 rows in st st.
Row 8: k1, [skpo] x 2, [k2tog] x 2, k6. (11 sts)
Row 9-13: work 5 rows in st st.
Row 14: k5, [m1, k3] x 2. (13 sts)
Row 15-23: work 9 rows in st st.
Row 24: k1, [k2tog] x 6. (7 sts)

Cut yarn, thread end through remaining sts, pull tight to gather. Sew up seam, leaving an opening. Stuff and sew closed.

Left arm
Begin at paw. CO 6 sts with MC.

Row 1: P 1 row.
Row 2: k1, [m1, k1] to end. (11 sts)
Row 3: P 1 row.
Row 4: [k2, m1] x 2, k3, [m1, k2] x 2. (15 sts)
Row 5-7: work 3 rows in st st.
Row 8: k6, [skpo] x 2, [k2tog] x 2, k1. (11 sts)
Row 9-13: work 5 rows in st st.

Panda
with a T-Shirt and a Super Cape

Row 14: [k3, m1] x 2, k5. (13 sts)
Row 15-23: work 9 rows in st st.
Row 24: k1, [k2tog] x 6. (7 sts)

Finish same as right arm.

Head

The intarsia section is marked with the yarn colour for each set of sts. Begin at back. CO 7 sts with CC.

Row 1: P 1 row.
Row 2: k1, [m1, k1] to end. (13 sts)
Row 3: P 1 row.
Row 4: k1, [m1, k1] to end. (25 sts)
Row 5-7: work 3 rows in st st.
Row 8: [k2, m1] x 4, k9, [m1, k2] x 4. (33 sts)
Row 9-15: work 7 rows in st st.
Row 16: CC k9, MC k3, CC k9, MC k3, CC k9.
Row 17: CC p8, MC p5, CC p7, MC p5, CC p8.
Row 18: CC k7, MC k7, CC k5, MC k7, CC k7.
Row 19: CC p6, MC p8, CC p5, MC p8, CC p6.
Row 20: CC k6, MC k8, CC k5, MC k8, CC k6.

Work rest of head in CC.

Row 21: P 1 row.
Row 22: k1, [skpo] x 7, k3, [k2tog] x 7, k1. (19 sts)
Row 23-25: work 3 rows in st st.
Row 26: k1, [k2tog] to end. (10 sts)

Cut yarn, thread end through remaining sts, pull tight to gather. Secure yarn ends from colour changes. Attach safety eyes. Sew up seam, leaving an opening. Stuff and sew closed. Make sure to put extra stuffing in the nose and cheeks.

Ears (make 2)

CO 3 sts with MC.

Row 1: P 1 row.
Row 2: k1, [m1, k1] x 2. (5 sts)
Row 3: P 1 row.
Row 4: k1, [m1, k1] x 4. (9 sts)
Row 5: P 1 row.
Row 6: k4, m1, k1, m1, k4. (11 sts)
Row 7-9: P 3 rows.
Row 10: k3, skpo, k1, k2tog, k3. (9 sts)
Row 11: P 1 row.
Row 12: [skpo] x 2, k1, [k2tog] x 2. (5 sts)
Row 13: P 1 row.
Row 14: skpo, k1, k2tog. (3 sts)

Cut yarn, thread end through remaining sts, pull tight to gather. Fold ear in half, with decreases to front and increases to back.

Finishing

If not using safety eyes, sew on button eyes, or embroider eyes with black yarn. With length of yarn, embroider nose and mouth. Sew ears in place on head (purl ridge is upper ear edge). Sew head securely to cast-on edge of body. Thread a length of yarn through left arm about 1 cm (¼") from top, thread yarn through body at shoulder position, then thread yarn through right arm. Thread yarn through body again, and then the left arm and pull tight. Repeat so yarn passes through each arm 3-4 times. Pull yarn tight so arms are secure, then fasten off yarn. Attach legs at lower edge of body in the same way as the arms.

T-Shirt

Materials

15 g of fingering or sport weight yarn, pair of 3 mm (US size 2.5) knitting needles, tapestry needle, 2 small buttons (optional).

Measurements

7 cm (2½") long, 19 cm (7") around.

Gauge/Tension

28 sts and 44 rows per 10 cm (4").

Front and Back

CO 30 sts.

Row 1-2: work 2 rows in k1, p1 rib.

Row 3-15: beginning with a P row, work 13 rows in st st.

Mark each end of row 15.

Row 16: k1, skpo, k to last 3 sts, k2tog, k1. (28 sts)

Row 17: P 1 row.

Row 18-19: repeat rows 16-17. (26 sts)

Row 20-29: work 10 rows in st st.

Row 30: Bind off 5 sts, k to end. (21 sts)

Row 31: Bind off 5 sts, [p1, k1] x 8. (16 sts)

Row 32: [p1, k1] x 8.

Bind off loosely in rib. Sew front to back along shoulder and neck band. To make the t-shirt easier to put-on and remove, you can leave one shoulder mostly open (you will need to sew a bit where the sleeves are attached). Then crochet a couple of button loops along the back edge, and sew the buttons to the front.

Sleeves

With right side facing you, pick up 22 sts between markers on front and back.

Row 1-4: work 5 rows in st st.
Row 6-7: [k1, p1] to end.

Bind off loosely in rib. Sew together side and underarm seams.

CAPE

Materials

15 g of worsted weight yarn, pair of 4.5 mm (US size 7) knitting needles, darning needle, tapestry hook (optional).

Measurements

9 cm (3½") long, 10 cm (4") wide.

Gauge

22 sts and 28 rows per 10 cm (4").

CO 23 sts.

Row 1-4: k1, [p1, k1] to end.
Row 5: k1, p1, k1, p17, k1, p1, k1.
Row 6: k1, p1, k19, p1, k1.
Row 7-25: repeat rows 5-6 x 9, then row 5 again.
Row 26: k1, p1, k1, [k2tog] x 4, k1, [skpo] x 4, k1, p1, k1. (15 sts)

Bind off all sts. Secure yarn ends. Braid or crochet 8 cm (3") ties at top corners of cape.

● ●

MONKEY

Materials

40 g of worsted weight yarn (MC), 10 g of contrasting worsted weight yarn (CC), yarn for embroidering face, two 8-10 mm buttons or safety eyes, stuffing, pair of 4 mm (US size 6) knitting needles, tapestry needle

Measurements

Approx. 20 cm (8") tall

Gauge/Tension

22 sts and 32 rows per 10 cm (4")

Legs (make 2)

CO 13 sts with MC.

Row 1: P 1 row.
Row 2: k1, [m1, k1] to end. (25 sts)
Row 3: P 1 row.
Row 4: [k2, m1, k3] x 5. (30 sts)
Row 5-9: work 5 rows in st st.
Row 10: k8, [k2tog] x 3, k2, [skpo] x 3, k8. (24 sts)
Row 11: P 1 row.
Row 12: k7, bind off 10 sts, k7. (14 sts)
Row 13-21: work 9 rows in st st.
Row 22: k1, skpo, k8, k2tog, k1. (12 sts)
Row 23-25: work 7 rows in st st.
Row 26: [k2tog] x 6. (6 sts)

MONKEY
with OVERALLS

Cut yarn, thread end through remaining sts, pull tight to gather. Sew top of foot together. Sew sole and back leg seam, leaving an opening. Stuff and sew closed.

Body

Begin at neck. CO 16 sts with MC.

Row 1: P 1 row.
Row 2: k1, [m1, k1] to end. (31 sts)
Row 3-5: work 3 rows in st st.
Row 6: k8, m1, k15, m1, k8. (33 sts)
Row 7-13: work 7 rows in st st.
Row 14: k15, m1, k3, m1, k15. (35 sts)
Row 15-17: work 3 rows in st st.
Row 18: k3, m1, k1, m1, k27, m1, k1, m1, k3. (39 sts)
Row 19: P 1 row.
Row 20: k16, skpo, k3, k2tog, k16. (37 sts)
Row 21-23: work 3 rows in st st.
Row 24: k15, skpo, k3, k2tog, k15. (35 sts)
Row 25-27: work 3 rows in st st.
Row 28: k1, [k2tog] to end. (18 sts)
Row 29: P 1 row.
Row 30: [k2tog] x 9. (9 sts)

Cut yarn, thread end through remaining sts, pull tight to gather. Sew up back seam to neck edge (leaving cast-on edge open). Stuff body.

Arms (make 2)

Begin at hand. CO 7 sts with CC.

Row 1: P 1 row.
Row 2: k1, [m1, k1] x 6. (13 sts)
Row 3-7: work 5 rows in st st.

Break off CC, start next row with MC.

Row 8-19: work 12 rows in st st.
Row 20: k1, skpo, k7, k2tog, k1. (11 sts)
Row 21-31: work 11 rows in st st.
Row 32: k1, [k2tog] x 5. (6 sts)

Cut yarn, thread end through remaining sts, pull tight to gather. Sew up seam, leaving an opening. Stuff and sew closed.

Head

The intarsia section is marked with the yarn colour for each set of sts. Begin at back of head. CO 7 sts with MC.

Row 1: P 1 row.
Row 2: k1, [m1, k1] to end. (13 sts)
Row 3: P 1 row.
Row 4: k1, [m1, k1] to end. (25 sts)
Row 5-7: work 3 rows in st st.
Row 8: [k2, m1] x 4, k9, [m1, k2] x 4. (33 sts)
Row 9-15: work 7 rows in st st.
Row 16: MC k12, CC k3, MC k3, CC k3, MC k12.
Row 17: MC p11, CC p5, MC p1, CC p5, MC p11.
Row 18: MC k11, CC k11, MC k11.
Row 19: MC p10, CC p13, MC p10.
Row 20: MC k10, CC k13, MC k10.

Work rest of head in CC.

Row 21: P 1 row.
Row 22: k2, [skpo] x 7, k1, [k2tog] x 7, k2. (19 sts)
Row 23: P 1 row.
Row 24: k7, skpo, k1, k2tog, k7. (17 sts)
Row 25-26: work 2 rows in st st.
Row 27: p1, [p2tog] x 8. (9 sts)

Cut yarn, thread end through remaining sts, pull tight to gather. Secure yarn ends from colour changes. Attach safety eyes. Sew up seam, leaving an opening. Stuff and sew closed. Make sure to put extra stuffing in the nose and cheeks.

Ears (make 2)

CO 7 sts with CC.

Row 1: P 1 row.
Row 2: skpo, k3, k2tog. (5 sts)
Row 3: p2tog, k1, p2tog tbl. (3 sts)

Cut yarn, thread end through remaining sts, pull tight to gather.

Tail

CO 8 sts with MC.

Work in st st for 5-6".

Cut yarn, thread end through remaining sts, pull tight to gather. Sew seam, adding a small amount of stuffing as you sew.

Finishing

If not using safety eyes, sew on button eyes, or embroider eyes with black yarn. With length of yarn, embroider nose and mouth. Sew ears in place on head (cast-on edge is outer ear edge). Sew head securely to cast-on edge of body. Thread a length of yarn through left arm about 1 cm (¼") from top, thread yarn through body at shoulder position, then thread yarn through right arm. Thread yarn through body again, and then the left arm and pull tight. Repeat so yarn passes through each arm 3-4 times. Pull yarn tight so arms are secure, then fasten off yarn. Attach legs at lower edge of body in the same way as the arms. Sew tail to monkey's bum.

OVERALLS

Materials

25 g of worsted weight yarn, pair of 4 mm (US size 6) knitting needles, tapestry needle, scrap yarn (optional: two 4 mm dpns, 2 small buttons)

Measurements

Approx 18 cm (7") around, 10 cm (4") long

Gauge/Tension

22 sts and 32 rows to 10 cm (4") in st st.

Left Leg

Begin at bottom of leg, end at waist. CO 24 sts.

Row 1: P 1 row.
Row 2: [k5, yo, k2tog, k5] x 2.
Row 3: P 1 row.
Row 4: kfb, k4, skpo, yo, k10, skpo, yo, k4, kfb. (26 sts)
Row 5: P 1 row.
Row 6: kfb, k5, yo, k2tog, k10, yo, k2tog, k5, kfb. (28 sts)
Row 7: P 1 row.

Mark each end of this row.

Row 8: k1, skpo, k4, skpo, yo, k10, skpo, yo, k4, k2tog, k1. (26 sts)
Row 9: P 1 row.
Row 10: k1, skpo, k3, yo, k2tog, k10, yo, k2tog, k3, k2tog, k1. (24 sts)
Row 11: P 1 row.
Row 12: [k5, skpo, yo, k5] x 2.
Row 13: P 1 row.
Row 14: [k5, yo, k2tog, k5] x 2.
Row 15-21: repeat rows 11-14, then rows 11-13 again.
Row 22: k6, [k2tog, k1] x 6. (18 sts)
Row 23: P 1 row.
Row 24: k2tog, k5, bind off 11 sts. (6 sts)

Place remaining sts on scrap yarn.

Right Leg

Follow pattern for left leg from row 1-21.

Row 22: [k1, skpo] x 6, k6. (18 sts)
Row 23: P 1 row.
Row 24: bind off 11 sts, k5, skpo. (6 sts)

Place remaining sts on scrap yarn. Sew together front seam of legs from waist to markers (leg fronts have live sts for bib).

Bib

Place sts from scrap yarn onto needle so WS is ready to knit (12 sts).

Row 1: s1, p11.
Row 2: s1, k11.
Row 3-9: repeat rows 1-2 x 3, then row 1 again.
Row 10: k3, bind off 6 sts, k3.

Straps

Worked as I-cord: transfer 3 sts to dpn. Work for 5 cm (2"). Bind off.
Worked flat: work in st st for 5 cm (2"), slipping first st of each row. Bind off.

Finishing

Sew together back seam of legs from waist edge to markers, leaving a small gap for the tail. If you want these to fit a bunny with a pom-pom tail, leave most of the back seam open, and attach an extra button and button loop at the waist to hold the back closed. Sew together crotch seam. Cross straps in back and sew ends to waistband. Sew buttons on bib corners.

PUG

Materials

100 g of tan chunky/bulky weight yarn (MC), 20 g of black or dark brown chunky/bulky weight yarn (CC), yarn for embroidering face, two 12-14 mm black buttons or safety eyes, stuffing, pair of 5 or 5.5 mm (US size 8 or 9) knitting needles, tapestry needle

Measurements

Approx. 30 cm (12") tall

Gauge/Tension

18 sts and 24 rows per 10 cm (4")

If you use chunky yarn for the pug, you will want to use 5 mm (US size 8) needles to knit it. If you use bulky yarn for the pug, you will want to use 5.5 mm (US size 9) needles.

Legs (make 2)

Begin at sole. CO 10 sts with MC.

Row 1: P 1 row.
Row 2: k1, [m1, k1] to end. (19 sts)
Row 3: P 1 row.
Row 4: k4, [m1, k3] x 5. (24 sts)
Row 5-9: work 5 rows in st st.
Row 10: k8, [skpo] x 2, [k2tog] x 2, k8. (20 sts)
Row 11: p6, [p2tog] x 2, [p2tog tbl] x 2, p6. (16 sts)
Row 12: k7, k2tog, k7. (15 sts)
Row 13-15: work 3 rows in st st.
Row 16: k2, m1, k11, m1, k2. (17 sts)
Row 17-25: work 9 rows in st st.
Row 26: k1, [k2tog] x 8. (9 sts)

Cut yarn, thread end through remaining sts, pull tight to gather. Sew sole and back leg seam, leaving an opening. Stuff and sew closed.

Body

Begin at neck. CO 17 sts with MC.

Row 1: P 1 row.
Row 2: k1, [m1, k1] to end. (33 sts)
Row 3-7: work 5 rows in st st.
Row 8: [k8, m1] x 2, k1, [m1, k8] x 2. (37 sts)
Row 9-15: work 7 rows in st st.
Row 16: k17, m1, k3, m1, k17. (39 sts)
Row 17-21: work 5 rows in st st.
Row 22: k4, m1, k1, m1, k29, m1, k1, m1, k4. (43 sts)
Row 23: P 1 row.
Row 24: k18, skpo, k3, k2tog, k18. (41 sts)
Row 25-27: work 3 rows in st st.
Row 28: k17, skpo, k3, k2tog, k17. (39 sts)
Row 29-31: work 3 rows in st st.
Row 32: K1, [k2tog] to end. (20 sts)
Row 33: P 1 row.
Row 34: [k2tog] to end. (10 sts)

Cut yarn, thread end through remaining sts, pull tight to gather. Sew up back seam to neck edge (leaving cast-on edge open). Stuff body.

Right arm

Begin at paw. CO 7 sts with MC.

Row 1: P 1 row.
Row 2: k1, [m1, k1] to end. (13 sts)
Row 3: P 1 row.
Row 4: k2, [m1, k3] x 3, m1, k2. (17 sts)
Row 5-9: work 5 rows in st st.
Row 10: k1, [skpo] x 2, k1, [k2tog] x 2, k7. (13 sts)
Row 11-15: work 5 rows in st st.
Row 16: k7, [m1, k3] x 2. (15 sts)

PUG
WITH AN ANORAK

Row 17-25: work 9 rows in st st.
Row 26: k1, [k2tog] x 7. (8 sts)

Cut yarn, thread end through remaining sts, pull tight to gather. Sew up seam, leaving an opening. Stuff and sew closed.

Left arm

Begin at paw. CO 7 sts with MC.

Row 1: P 1 row.
Row 2: k1, [m1, k1] to end. (13 sts)
Row 3: P 1 row.
Row 4: k2, [m1, k3] x 3, m1, k2. (17 sts)
Row 5-9: work 5 rows in st st.
Row 10: k7, [skpo] x 2, k1, [k2tog] x 2, k1. (13 sts)
Row 11-15: work 5 rows in st st.
Row 16: [k3, m1] x 2, k7. (15 sts)
Row 17-25: work 9 rows in st st.
Row 26: k1, [k2tog] x 7. (8 sts)

Finish same as right arm.

Head

The intarsia section is marked with the yarn colour for each set of sts. Begin at back. CO 8 sts with MC.

Row 1: P 1 row.
Row 2: k1, [m1, k1] to end. (15 sts)
Row 3: P 1 row.
Row 4: k1, [m1, k1] to end. (29 sts)
Row 5-7: work 3 rows in st st.
Row 8: [k3, m1] x 3, k11, [m1, k3] x 3. (35 sts)
Row 9-18: work 10 rows in st st.
Row 19: MC p11, CC p3, MC p7, CC p3, MC p11.
Row 20: MC k3, k2tog, k2, m1, k3, CC k5, MC k2tog, m1, k1, m1, skpo, CC k5, MC k3, m1, k2, skpo, k3.
Row 21: MC p10, CC p5, MC p5, CC p5, MC p10.
Row 22: MC k3, k2tog, k2, m1, k3, CC k5, MC k2tog, m1, k1, m1, skpo, CC k5, MC k3, m1, k2, skpo, k3.
Row 23: MC P 1 row.

Work rest of head in CC.

Row 24: [k1, k2tog] x 4, k11, [skpo, k1] x 4. (27 sts)

Row 25: P 1 row.
Row 26: [k4, k2tog] x 2, k3, [skpo, k4] x 2. (23 sts)
Row 27: P 1 row.
Row 28: k3, k2tog, k13, skpo, k3. (21 sts)
Row 29: P 1 row.
Row 30: [k2tog] x 5, k1, [skpo] x 5. (11 sts)

Cut yarn, thread end through remaining sts, pull tight to gather. Secure yarn ends from colour changes. Attach safety eyes. Fold nose end up between eyes and stitch in place with CC yarn. Sew up seam, leaving an opening. Stuff and sew closed. Make sure to put extra stuffing in the nose and cheeks.

Ears (make 2)

CO 3 sts with CC.

Row 1: K 1 row.
Row 2: k1, [m1, k1] x 2. (5 sts).
Row 3: K 1 row.
Row 4: k1, m1, k to end. (6 sts)
Row 5: K 1 row.
Row 6-11: repeat rows 4-5 x 3. (9 sts)
Row 12-15: K 4 rows in garter st.
Row 16: k1, skpo, k to last 3 sts, k2tog, k1. (7 sts)
Row 17: K 1 row.
Row 18-19: repeat rows 16-17. (5 sts)
Row 20: k1, s1, k2tog, psso, k1. (3 sts)
Row 21: K 1 row.

Cut yarn, thread end through remaining stitches, pull tight to gather.

Tail

CO 15 sts with MC.

Row 1: P 1 row.
Row 2: [k2, m1] x 7, k1. (22 sts)
Row 4: [k3, m1] x 7, k1. (29 sts)
Row 5: P 1 row.
Row 6: [k2, k2tog] x 7, k1. (22 sts)
Row 7: P 1 row.
Row 8: [k1, k2tog] x 7, k1. (15 sts)
Row 9: P 1 row.

Bind off. Sew bound off edge to CO edge, adding stuffing as you sew, and sew closed one end of tail.

Finishing

If not using safety eyes, sew on button eyes, or embroider eyes with black yarn. With length of yarn, embroider nose and mouth. Attach ears: sew ear edge with increases to side of head. Sew head securely to cast-on edge of body. Thread a length of yarn through left arm about 1 cm (¼") from top, thread yarn through body at shoulder position, then thread yarn through right arm. Thread yarn through body again, and then the left arm and pull tight. Repeat so yarn passes through each arm 3-4 times. Pull yarn tight so arms are secure, then fasten off yarn. Attach legs at lower edge of body in the same way as the arms. Sew open end of tail to pug's bum.

ANORAK

Materials

50 g of worsted weight yarn, 4 mm (US size 6) circular needle, 4 st markers, scrap yarn, tapestry needle, button or ribbon (optional)

If your toy is much bigger than 30 cm (12"), use 4.5 mm (US size 7) needle, and you may need more than 50 g of yarn.

Measurements

28 cm (11") around, 10 cm (4") long excluding hood

Gauge/Tension

22 sts and 28 rows per 10 cm (4")

Garment is worked flat, except for sleeves, if you wish to knit them in the round.

Hood

CO 48 sts.

Row 1-4: K 4 rows in garter st.
Row 5-17: beginning with a P row, work 13 rows in st st.
Row 18: k31, k3tog tbl, turn.
Row 19: s1, p14, p3tog, turn.
Row 20: s1, k14, k3tog tbl, turn.
Row 21: s1, p14, p3tog, turn.
Row 22: s1, k14, ssk, turn.
Row 23: s1, p14, p2tog, turn.

Repeat rows 22-23 until 16 sts remain (you should end on a WS row).

Yoke

Pick up 10 sts along hood edge, with last st at CO edge. (26 sts)

Row 1: k26, pick up 10 sts along other hood edge. (36 sts)
Row 2: k3, p30, k3.
Row 3: k3, [m1, k2] x 15, m1, k3. (52 sts)
Row 4: k3, p6, PM, p9, PM, p16, PM, p9, PM, p6, k3.
Row 5: k8, m1, k1, SM, k1, m1, k7, m1, k1, SM, k1, m1, k14, m1, k1, SM, k1, m1, k7, m1, k1, SM, k1, m1, k8. (60 sts)
Row 6: k3, p to last 3 sts, k3.
Row 7-16: On RS rows, continue to increase 1 st before and after each marker, adding total of 8 sts per increase row, until you have 100 sts.

Body

Row 17: k14, kfb, place 21 sts on scrap yarn, k27, kfb, place 21 sts on scrap yarn, k15. (60 sts)
Row 18: k3, p54, k3.
Row 19: K 1 row.
Next: Repeat rows 18-19 x 3 (or x 5 for a longer body)
Next: Work 3 rows of garter st, then bind off.

Sleeves worked flat

Place 21 sts from scrap yarn onto needle so RS is ready to knit.

Row 1: kfb, k19, kfb. (23 sts)
Next: Work 7 rows in st st (or 9 rows for longer sleeves)
Next: Work 3 rows in garter st, then bind off. Sew underarm seams.

Sleeves worked in the round

Place 21 sts from scrap yarn onto needle so RS is ready to knit.

Round 1: Pick up 1 st in underarm, k21. (22 sts)
Round 2: k2tog, k20. (21 sts)
Next: Work 6 rounds in st st (or 8 rounds for longer sleeves)
Next: Work 3 rows in garter st, then bind off.

Secure all yarn ends, and close up any holes under arms. To finish, add a button loop and button, crocheted or ribbon ties, or even a zipper if you're feeling ambitious.

ABBREVIATIONS

CO = cast on
[…] x N = repeat sequence in brackets N times ("to end" means repeat until the end of the row)
K or **k** = knit
c1b = worked on next 2 sts on left needle: k into back of second st, then k into front of first st, then slip both off left needle
c1f = worked on next 2 sts on left needle: k into front of second st, then k into back of first st, then slip both off left needle
k2tog = decrease 1 by knitting 2 together
k3tog = decrease 2 by knitting 3 together, same technique as k2tog
kfb = increase 1 by knitting into front, then back of next stitch
m1 = increase 1 by picking up loop between stitch just worked and next stitch, and knit into the back of this loop
P or **p** = purl
p2tog = decrease 1 by purling 2 together
p3tog = decrease 2 by purling 3 together, same technique as p2tog
PM = place marker
psso = pass slipped stitch over stitch just worked
RS = right side
s1 = slip 1 st from left needle to right needle
s2 = slip 2 sts, as if to k2tog
skpo = slip 1, knit 1, pass slipped stitch over
SM = slip marker
ssk = decrease 1 by s1, s1 purl-wise, knit slipped sts together
st or **sts** = stitch or stitches
st st = stocking stitch
tbl = through back of loop(s)
WS = wrong side
yo = yarn over

Copyright © 2010 by Barbara Prime & Konstantin Ryabitsev
ISBN: 978-0-9811393-1-9

Selling toys? Sharing patterns? Sure! Just a few rules:
http://fuzzymitten.com/sharing-and-selling.html

www.ingramcontent.com/pod-product-compliance
Lightning Source LLC
Chambersburg PA
CBHW042339150426
43195CB00001B/40